Praise for *And Then It Just Got Worse*

"In years to come, the tragicomedy of the Cancellation Era—the one still leaving the wounded and the dead in its wake—will also be known by the books written by those who suffered, raged, then wrote about their experience. Ted Royer is at the head of the pack."

—Bruce Wagner, author

"This book isn't just an account of cancellation—it's a testament to the quiet resilience of those who refuse to stay broken."

—Jennifer Sey, author of *Levi's Unbuttoned* and *Chalked Up*

"An important story well told by someone with the true grit to have survived it—and with the insight, humor, and determination to share it the right way."

—Mark Halperin, journalist and bestselling author of *Game Change*

AND THEN IT JUST GOT WORSE

AND THEN IT JUST GOT WORSE

Blundering Through Cancellation, Advertising, and the Wrong Side of #MeToo

TED ROYER

Skyhorse Publishing

Skyhorse Publishing books may be purchased in bulk at special discounts for sales promotion, corporate gifts, fundraising, or educational purposes. Special editions can also be created to specifications. For details, contact the Special Sales Department, Skyhorse Publishing, 307 Fifth Avenue, 4th Floor, New York, NY 10016 or info@skyhorsepublishing.com.

Skyhorse® and Skyhorse Publishing® are registered trademarks of Skyhorse Publishing, Inc.®, a Delaware corporation.

Visit our website at www.skyhorsepublishing.com.

10 9 8 7 6 5 4 3 2 1

Library of Congress Congress Control Number: 2026940062

Cover design by Ralph Watson
Cover photo credit: Ralph Watson

Print ISBN: 978-1-5107-8667-7
Ebook ISBN: 978-1-5107-8668-4

Printed in the United States of America

Dedicated to everyone who deserved better.

Contents

There are really only two reasons to write: desperation or revenge.

—ELIZABETH HARDWICK

The Roof

It's 1:00 a.m., and I am sitting on the roof of my building. It's a nice roof. A combination of wood pavers and flagstone surfaces surrounded by a few brick walls and low metal railings. The railings are so low that the building has a rule for kids: do not touch the railings, ever. I can proudly take some credit for its niceness, as I was on my building's Roof Committee. We made good decisions, putting in planters and new umbrellas over the tables. It all looks clean and beautiful. But I'm not here as a member of the Roof Committee.

I'm here to jump.

My building is six stories tall. The view is great. Most of the surrounding ones are taller but of varying heights, and Tribeca has a lot of buildings this tall or a little taller, so I can see a lot of the neighborhood from here. I can see the Woolworth building. I can just see the Hudson River. And, of course, the Freedom Tower looms large to my right. I have no idea exactly how tall this building is, but the average six-story building is between sixty and ninety feet high. That height is no guarantee that I will die, but this is the only roof I have access to. At the moment that I am on the roof, I work at an agency in a much taller building, but I do not want to kill myself at work. That seems to me, at this moment, unnecessarily selfish.

I am using this roof because it's here now, and I am in the middle of a suicidal red zone, known by psychologists as the Suicidal Deliberation period or the Active Stage. I know about this because I did an ad campaign about suicide prevention. I've read all about this. People get depressed and think about killing themselves in the Suicidal Ideation period. But it gets real when they enter the Active Stage. That's when you stop thinking about it and decide to go for it. No more fucking around, let's do this, now.

The edge of the roof is about nine feet away. I am sitting this far back from it to guard against any sudden emotional impulse: if I do this, I want to be sure I have decided to do it, not just followed an impulse. I am protecting myself from my brain taking action and making me jump against my will.

It is cold. My eyes are filled with tears from the cold, but I am not crying. I am calm. So calm that there's a part of me that's scared by how calm I feel. The scared part is looking at the stronger, more in-control calm part and noticing the growing sense of determination. That's why I'm scared.

I do not want to live like this anymore.

Outside of my brain, I lead a good life. I lead a privileged life. Society reminds me of this all the time. It tells me relentlessly how privileged I am. I have a beautiful, loyal, funny wife who I know loves me. I have two children who are smart, healthy, and adorable. I have enough money to not starve. I have some very loyal friends, most of whom remind me of how lucky I am. I have a community around me in the neighborhood that is there for us when we need them.

Later, after I do not jump, I will read a lot more about suicide. Apparently, the better one's life, the more suicidal one can be, because the falling from a beautiful life to a life of despair is such an enormous fall. This from *Scientific American*:

> Idealistic conditions actually heighten suicide risk because they often create unreasonable standards for personal happiness, thereby rendering people more emotionally fragile in response to unexpected setbacks. So, when things get a bit messy, such people, many of whom appear to have led mostly privileged lives, have a harder time coping with failures.
>
> [Psychologist Roy] Baumeister tells us that "It is apparently the size of the discrepancy between standards and perceived reality that is crucial for initiating the suicidal process." It's the proverbial law of social gravity: the higher your majesty is to start off with, the more painful it's going to be when you happen to fall flat on your face.[1]

Later, after not jumping, this makes perfect sense: my majesty was fucking high. Thus, I am staring at the edge of the building. And while I stare at the edge, I am trying as hard as I can to zero in on everything I am feeling that makes me want to walk over, step up onto the low railing, and dive headfirst down to the street. (At sixty to ninety feet, it has to be headfirst; otherwise I could just break my legs.) This reason to jump must be a good enough reason to jump. So, I'm going to use what could be my last few minutes to really evaluate *hard.* My brain owes it to me.

I am not feeling loneliness, although I do feel lonely a lot these days. I am not feeling physical pain, despite my back and stomach knotting with regularity. Otherwise, I am not in chronic pain. Chronic, debilitating pain is a totally valid reason to want to kill oneself. I am not feeling regret. I have lived my life in a way that I knew was sometimes reckless but was also filled with laughter and real connections and great conversations. I don't regret my life at all.

I find it. I identify what I am feeling. I am feeling *shame.*

That's it. Shame. I zero in on the feeling of shame and roll around in it. I don't just feel shame; I live in it. It's constant. I'm drowning in it every day, every hour. Shame for hurting people.

Shame for the humiliation I went through. Shame for the life I could have had but lost. Shame for the massive, awful, twisting calamity I have gone through. With everyone seeing it, everyone knowing about it. Everyone, *everyone,* I know.

How do I know that shame and not some mental predisposition is the cause of this suicidality? Because shame is a new feeling. At least shame at this level. Before this shame, I was a happy person who never once considered suicide an option. Never. I loved life. No matter how bad it got, I knew that friends, family, and the world in general held too much goodness for checking out to be anywhere near an option. Now, on the roof, life holds very little appeal.

Later, after not jumping, I will also research shame. According to psychologist Robert Karen and the *Atlantic*, there are four types of shame: existential, situational, class, and narcissistic:

> **Existential shame** occurs when we become self-aware of an objective, unpleasant truth about ourselves or our situation. **Situational shame** is the feeling we have when violating an ethical principle, interpersonal boundary, or cultural norm. **Class shame** relates to social power and pertains to skin color, social class, ethnic background, and gender and occurs in societies that have rigid caste stratifications or disparate classes. **Narcissistic shame** occurs when our self-image and pride are wounded, affecting how we feel and think about ourselves as an individual, in contrast to as a member of a group.[2]

Existential shame? Existentially, yes, I will never be free of this situation, ever. Situationally, of course: I am considered a sexual harasser. I have stepped on one of society's biggest land mines and it has blown me up. I have made choices deemed by today's world to be horrible and unforgivable. I have hurt someone. I don't know who, and I don't know specifically which of my actions or comments hurt them, but I've been told I hurt someone so I must have hurt someone.

Class shame? I guess. I am an older white man, and therefore, unlike, say, Lizzo, society does not want to forgive me. I have been deemed unredeemable. I am now a disposable person. Narcissistic shame? Duh. My entire conception of myself has been shattered. I've always sort of hated myself in a low-level, able-to-cover-it-with-drugs-alcohol-and-hedonism way; now my self-hatred has been set free, grown exponentially powerful, and is pretty much running things. If this were the Shame Justice League, I am Superman. This is alpha shame.

Later, after not jumping, I will recognize that I am feeling all four types of shame. I'm swimming in a deep pool of existential dread, situational agony, class contempt, and narcissism. To me, at this moment, they aren't separate, but an all-encompassing swirl of shame, and the swirl is strong enough to infiltrate every nook and cranny of my mind and soul. As I stare at the ledge, I try to give shape to it. I think of Dr. Seuss's *Oh, The Places You'll Go!*, visualizing the page where the hero is eyeball-to-eyeball with a huge green monster. That illustration represents the nadir of his life, his worst moment ever.

I've read this book to my kids a hundred times. After being fired, that page really hit hard. Yes, the monster was huge, and the cave was dark. But the little guy was patting him on the nose, dismissing the monster as if he were no big deal. What the fuck, Seuss? Were you promising that life's biggest problems would be so easy that you could pat them on the nose?

This problem of mine is massive, because this shame cannot be patted on the nose. This shame is life-changing, permanently. This is cancer-causing shame.* I am in a shame storm. My shame

* I have a totally unfounded theory that horrible, never-ending negative emotions can cause cancer. There is, to my knowledge, little-to-zero concrete scientific evidence for this.

storm is like the planet Jupiter. Jupiter has storms all over its surface. It looks serene from afar, but Jupiter is pretty much made of storms.

My reality is telling me the only way to escape this shame storm is to jump.

I close my eyes and again go over the consequences of jumping. I have been rolling these around at various times for months, and I methodically work through them all now as best I can through the torrential noise in my head.*

The first consequence I consider is financial. My wife and kids will be OK. I have decent savings and can leave them enough money to keep going. Over the months I have been thinking about this, tallying what I can leave for them, whether it will be enough to make my decision fiscally responsible. Remove me from the picture and the money goes considerably further.

The second consideration is my extended family. I have been to a couple of family funerals lately. My extended family is great, but we are not extremely close. My loss will hurt, but only for a while; it will fade, and they will move on with their own lives, more quickly than I want to admit.

The third is my friends. Same thing. But I have been to more than a couple funerals of friends (not suicides, btw), and people move on. The impact will fade—again, more quickly than I want to admit. Also, I've had some solid experience in seeing just how easily friends let someone fade from their lives. This experience makes the decision to jump that much more compelling. Also from *Scientific American*:

* It must be noted that very little about this moment was logical, despite how I present it here. The reality is that it was a mess of ugly thoughts whipping around, not in any semblance of order at all. Only in writing this now can I (sort of) organize it into a sequence of thoughts.

> When they do mention significant others, suicide note writers usually speak of them as being cut off, distant, separate, not understanding, or opposed. Friends and family, even a loving mother at arm's length, feel endless oceans away.[3]

Yep. They are oceans away now. And as if to rub it in, I saw the following paragraph on TikTok before coming up to the roof. The author is unknown and there are many versions. It's about dying, and its different iterations have thousands of views and positive comments:

> Do you know what will happen after your funeral? After a few hours, the crying will stop. Your family will be busy ordering food from hotels and caterers for relatives. The crowd will start to dissolve. Some will go to the nearby pub for a drink before going to bed. A relative will apologize for not being able to come because of an emergency. Foreign relatives will have secretly planned a trip around the funeral.
>
> In the coming days your phone will receive a few texts or emails from people who don't know you're dead. People will search you on social out of morbid curiosity to see what your last post was.
>
> After a month your wife will be watching a comedy show and she will laugh.
>
> Everybody's life will go back to normal.
>
> One day, looking at some old photos, one of your close friends will think about you.
>
> People are waiting to forget you easily. Are you living to satisfy them? Life is once; just live it.

Now, I know this is meant to be inspirational, but fuck me if this isn't a *great* advertisement for suicide. *If you're dead, then nothing matters*. Lying in bed at night, doom scrolling and feeling like killing myself, this was not a good video to find. For weeks afterward, I couldn't get the thought out of my head: *Everyone will get over it. More quickly than you think.*

The urge to jump, the urge to swerve off the road, the urge to take too many pills isn't constant. It surges up and recedes, like waves or volcanic activity. The volcano thing is more accurate. The pressure builds under what seems like a calm surface, and when it bursts up it does so violently, propelled by the unstable elements underneath. The thought of killing oneself can burn bright and hot in contrast to the seemingly peaceful day-to-day routine. It hides under normalcy, because you don't want to freak anyone out. And you don't want to freak yourself out. Maintain. Maintain.*

Tonight, on the roof, the urge bubbled and burst and covered the Roof Committee's work with lava.

"So jump," an inner voice told me.

My wife will be OK. She is beautiful and funny and resilient. She will be damaged, but she will go on. She is incredibly strong. This determination is quick and decisive. She will go on.

My kids will be OK. They are young enough to rebound. My father died when I was fourteen. It was terrible, but I moved past it. They will go on.

Have you ever read about a person who not only kills themself but takes their family with them? Happens all the time; you would know this if you read the *Daily Mail* every day like I do. Let's say a man kills his whole family before committing suicide. It's the ultimate selfish move. In the comments section of such articles,

---

* The best example of this can be found in an ad for #worldmentalhealthday from the Norwich City Football club. Simple and powerful. I'm jealous as hell of this ad, and that really is a creative's highest praise. I won't describe it here. I recommend looking it up on YouTube.

people say, "How can someone do this? I don't understand." Yet . . . I think I understand. The life the suicidal man was building was no longer ahead of him. He may have lost his fortune or otherwise been disgraced or affected by something equally awful. He has entered a new, much worse version of his life. That previous great life included his family and now the future shitty life *also* includes his family. He's blown it for all of them. They have been robbed of a great life just as much as he has. He can't go on, and he knows whatever life they go on with won't be nearly as good as the former life he had planned. If he kills himself, that new bad life will become that much worse for his family; they'll have a dead father and husband on top of their diminished existence. So, the best route is to end it for everybody. *If you're dead, then nothing matters.*

I want to be unequivocal here: the thought of harming others *never* enters into my calculations. I understand the logic of this while fully understanding it is monstrous and selfish. I map it out because I am looking at the ledge and I am *making calculations.* I am calculating possible outcomes, possible realities. I am surprised by how logical my calculations are becoming in a moment of emotional pain. I have only empathy and understanding for others who have packed it in.

But at some point, somewhere in the back of my head, I am calculating because I know these calculations can save me. Logic may be my only way out of the storm. I am spinning the narrative, and this is a way to turn the spin into something I can control. A + B = C. A + B + C = D. A + B + C + D = not dying.

The danger is that logic can also swing against me: *If you're dead, then nothing matters. Nothing.* This thought starts winning again. It is logically true and emotionally true at the same time. It is so much more powerful. It's a suicide trump card.

Then the storm rises up, once again, against the one projection onto the future that I dismissed before but can't logically or emotionally navigate my way around now: The only real effect of my suicide will be to irreparably harm my children's lives. It will devastate them now, in the near future, and in the far future. It will be carried by them forever. My suicide is their life sentence.

This thought becomes much stronger. So, I work it. I build it up. I picture my son and my daughter, devastated and sobbing. I visualize them in therapy. I see them through the decades, the background of their lives ever shaded in sadness and uncertainty. In response, the storm rages back: *Their pain won't matter. If you're dead, then nothing matters.*

Then I come up with a response: By killing myself, I might be giving them permission to kill themselves in the future.

The battle isn't over, but this is the decisive turning point. I have never had this thought before; it's fresh and new: *I might be giving my children permission to kill themselves.* The storm winds cannot rip out the bolts and beams from this one. It isn't just a thought anymore, it's concrete, it's reality. I am willing it into being reality.

The shame remains. The twisting in my guts goes on. But the gusts are waning. I am just now realizing that I am breathing heavily in a sort of self-soothing rhythm. My face is cold. I get up and leave the roof. The light in the hallway is bright and judgmental. The descent down to my apartment makes me feel melodramatic and embarrassed. The memory of the roof is already becoming fuzzy. Like getting up and walking away from the table after a Monopoly game is over, what was so real and important a half hour ago feels stupid and trivial. Was I in the Active Stage? Or am I even so pathetic that I was just going through some weird motions?

In the aftermath, I feel this new shame, shame that I *didn't* do it, that I wasn't brave enough to follow through. And then even more shame that I had even remotely considered doing this at all, shame that I considered for even a moment leaving my children.

From now on, until I actually do die, I am Jupiter: always a storm raging somewhere.

*Nodus Tollens**: January 3, 2018

"There's a list of sexual harassers that just came out. You're on the top of it."

With that sentence, a hole in the ground began to open beneath me. With that sentence, years of pain, loss, loneliness, financial ruin, self-discovery, spirituality, and stormy ideas—the constant conflict between whether to end it and how to keep going on—began.

I had just come back from a trip to Australia for the holidays with my family. Not a great trip; the jet lag had been bad and my wife and I had been fighting a lot. Add to that two young kids, an intense career with a work schedule that never turned off, and an almost total lack of exercise. I had become irritable with such a load. But it was a new year, and I was determined it was going to be a great one.

* Is there anything more pretentious than starting off with a Latin phrase, especially this early in the book? It may alleviate the pretension (and your annoyance) to know that I too just learned this phrase. According to *The Dictionary of Obscure Sorrows*, it means "the realization that the plot of your life doesn't make sense to you—that although you were following the arc of the story, you keep finding yourself immersed in passages you don't understand, that don't even seem to belong in the same genre." That's pretty good.

Now I was on set in Santa Monica, shooting the last few scenes of, funnily enough, an Australian tourism campaign. We were filming Margot Robbie in a scene where she plays a tough woman from the outback. The concept revolved around a fake film reboot of *Crocodile Dundee*; we were shooting trailers and promos with all the bells and whistles to make it appear that a real film was coming out. In addition to Robbie, our leading stars were Chris Hemsworth and Danny McBride, with whom we had worked the previous November. The plan was that, during the Super Bowl, what seemed to be a trailer for the new *Crocodile Dundee* would be revealed as a tourism ad, much to the disappointment of McBride, who acted like he had been led to believe he would be starring in an actual movie. It was big and silly and meta all at the same time, my favorite kind of idea.

We were in the video village, a set-up for agency creatives to watch the filming without getting in the way of the director, watching Robbie do her scenes. Obviously, she was a pro, and the whole thing was going smoothly. My phone rang. The voice on the other end belonged to someone I had worked with, on and off, for decades.

"Hey, the shoot is going really great. You're going to love it."

"Good. Listen . . ."

The voice said it. Sexual harassment. Top of the list. My hands felt like they were inflating with air, my mouth dried instantly, and my head felt packed in cotton.

"Oh fuck. Fuck."

"Yeah, it's not good."

"Fuck. What can I do? What can we do?"

"We'll try to protect you, but we have to protect the agency."

With that sentence I knew I was fired.

Droga5 didn't play around when its reputation and fortune were being messed with. In eleven years, we had built an ad agency from scratch to become one of—if not *the*—most creatively successful in the world. I joined six months after the founding of Droga5, and it had become my entire life. We had won countless awards, grown to employ more than 750 people, and been named Cannes Independent Agency of the Year three years in a row. Colleagues there had become some of my best friends. Going to work was a joy. It was always hard work, but the best kind of hard work: focused and passionate, with inspiring, creative ideas always at the core.

All of that began disappearing during this phone call.

It went on for a few more minutes, but I don't remember any of it. Everything was a blank. I could barely see or hear anything right in front of me. My mouth didn't seem capable of speech. I went back to the shoot and faked my way through the day. Occasionally there would be calls with our PR director, our HR director, others, all trying to reassure me that it would be OK. None of them sounded remotely convinced of what they were saying.

This was early 2018. Does anyone reading this remember that time? I mean, really remember it? The atmosphere was explosive. #MeToo was coming for advertising, an industry known for its drinking, drugs, and affairs. *Mad Men* wasn't far off when depicting what the ad world was like. The industry had been braced for months for the coming "reckoning." People were not only giddy with speculation over who would go down, but also intensely paranoid about any of their past transgressions being dragged out into the light. "Delete the previous text" was a very common text message. As author Noah Rothman put it, "Cancellation is so widely discussed because so many recognize that it could happen to them as well."

Did I deserve what was headed my way? Maybe. *Maybe* meaning that I was just as deserving as the average person in the industry, for sure. Advertising had been a playground for me. I had emotional affairs and hook-ups. I got high with so many people.

Award shows were drunken messes. The hard-partying lifestyle seemed to be inextricably intertwined with the intensity of business wins, financial success, and industry recognition. Now there was a collective realization that we had been acting irresponsibly for too long.

In 1994 I went to my first ad party, thrown by a creative director of an agency whose name I won't mention. I was a student from the ad school called the Portfolio Center, in this new town trying to get into this agency, one of the best in the world. I walked into the party and immediately noticed the thick cloud of marijuana smoke and coke lines being laid out on the coffee table. A couple was making out in a corner. "They're married," someone said, then added, "Not to each other, of course." This was my introduction to the ad world. It seemed crazy, free, creative, random, sometimes dangerous, sometimes lucrative, but most of all really, really fun.

Back to the shoot. When it ended for the day, our client hugged me and said, "You were on fire today! Thank you!" I barely remembered anything that had happened in the previous hours at all. My autopilot had done well.

I took a car back to the hotel. My wife greeted me at our door with a face as shocked and ashen as my own. She knew. The list was spreading all over social media. Everyone we knew and everyone else in advertising was watching, sharing, and joking as our lives collapsed.

We hugged, both crying, and slumped onto the floor as the hole in the ground opened wide. Together we fell into it.

Belated Introduction

Showing your emotions to people is like bleeding next to sharks.

—BRAZILIAN PROVERB

Apologies in advance, because for the next few minutes—actually, for most of this book—I'm going to bleed all over you. Buckets.

I am writing this introduction eight years later. Eight years of the strongest emotional pain I've ever come close to feeling, constant and pervasive, the long COVID of emotional pain.

MeToo: No one wants to hear about your pain.

Say hello to the personification of #MeToo that lives in my head. I'm going to do something risky, but in doing so I'm stealing from the best: Socrates. In my life, the voice of #MeToo pops up in my head daily to debate and argue with me, and to keep me in check. So I personify it here to talk with it. I recognize that it is perhaps incredibly problematic for an aging white male to personify such a voice, but I want to stress that in no way is it meant to represent women or their point of view. The voice I hear and write is a characterization of what I've absorbed and learned from books, articles, real conversations, Twitter posts, Diet Madison Avenue's (DMA) very aggressive and cruel commentary, and articles from sites like Jezebel. Anywhere and everywhere I can, really. Mostly, it's a voice shaped in my head from over a hundred conversations I set out to have with women after I got fired. They have been by turns sympathetic and empathetic, fiercely critical of and highly analytical toward the person I was and am, my behavior, and my impact on them individually, as well as the impact on people around me. All of those conversations and more have distilled themselves into the powerful, sharp, sometimes scary, sometimes impatient, no-bullshit voice that I have in my head. As for MeToo's first line, "*No one wants to hear your pain,*" I heard this exact line spoken to my face. A lot. From women. From women who were close friends. Imagine being in the worst pain of your life and hearing this. The #MeToo movement was and is of huge importance, but still, ouch.

When we talk, I will do my best to remain fair-minded. Often, I lose arguments to MeToo. I want you to know that, despite the joshing and joking directions these conversations go, I take this extremely seriously, more seriously than I've ever taken anything in my life.

MeToo: Do you?
Ted: Can we get into it later? I promise we will. Just right now, it's important to establish the introduction; it affects the journey later.
MeToo: OK, let me know when you've finished complaining, I really don't need to read an aging white man's complaints in a world full of so much more undeserved pain than yours.
Ted: That's fair. I will definitely let you know.

And now it's eight years later. Things are still bad. Recently, I was told that a freelance job I was doing for a company has been cancelled because some younger staff members heard I was working on it (more on this later). This company is headquartered in California and I am in New York City. I was nowhere near their office, yet the mention of my name drove the staff to revolt and, when company meetings were held, to shake and cry. This happened. No one there knows what I have actually done. Because I don't know what I actually did. Oh, I know some things. But they aren't #MeToo-able things. And they aren't the things that the online group called Diet Madison Avenue accused me of (more on that later). Because those things didn't happen.

In 2018 I was fired. I tried to freelance and was hounded out of that job. I was offered jobs and then faced internal objections that killed the offers. I resigned from the board of the One Club, a position I'd had for years in an advertising creative organization I loved dearly. I dropped out of several high-profile speaking engagements and judging gigs. And for the next eight years, I scraped together a meager living that was a fraction of what I had earned before.

Today, I live in a strange world where, at home, my family acts as if life is normal. My children get the bulk of our attention. Our community, neighborhood, and their schools constitute most of our social lives. Here I am treated as just another dad, and though I am aware of murmurs about me (and some people have asked me straight up about my #MeToo experience), no one seems to judge me for it. In fact, it's probably served as an invitation for others to open up more about their struggles and experiences. We live in Manhattan . . .

MeToo: Oh God. you live in Manhattan and you're complaining about life.
Ted: I thought you were waiting to let me finish this part.
MeToo: It's like a car crash. I can't look away. The narcissism and self-pity are overwhelming.

Ted: Well, it's my life. When you're living in it, the advantages, the privileges, aren't as . . . can we hold off? So much, later on, is about gratitude and growth. I promise, I grow. Please?

MeToo: Please, by all means, continue.

We live in a nice neighborhood. The people who we know also know about me. Some of them are rich. Some of them are rich as fuck. Keeping up with the Joneses can be very intimidating when surrounded by venture capitalists and Goldman Sachs bankers. It's impossible for me to keep up now. I'm struggling to hold onto our place. However, my vulnerability and shame seem to humanize me somehow to them, and they are uniformly nice about my cancellation. If I make anyone uncomfortable here, I've never seen it.

But I also live in a world where people hate and fear me, to the point that the mere mention of my name or my walking into a room can set someone alight with anger or make them tear up in outrage. I went to an ad party soon after being fired, and while I was mostly embraced by my friends and acquaintances, I was also met with the following statements:

"I think it's disgusting that you are here."

"If I could, I would hurt you more than you've already been hurt."

"You should never be allowed to come to another party like this again."

The online comments are orders-of-magnitude worse. Online, I live in a world where I almost don't exist at all professionally. I avoid LinkedIn, and I almost never check Facebook. I have several Instagram accounts that are not at all ad related. These accounts are private, and I mute the people who post about advertising. I just don't want to see, or be seen by, my old industry. When I see someone bragging about new work, or announcing a promotion or some other success, a hot flush rolls over my body, and I'm temporarily gripped by a mixture of sadness, jealousy, and anger. It passes after a moment, but it still stings.

Has it mellowed out after eight years?

Yes and no. Yes, in that the people who seem to want to get past it with me don't bring it up as often. They get embarrassed when acknowledging it. Some don't know whether to confront it out of the gate or avoid it. The invitations to lunch so that I can be gawked at like a circus freak have dried up. I get trickles of work. Most people are probably bored with it. Someone else's pain gets boring. But I get very stark reminders that my #MeToo reputation is alive and well, and you will read about them in this book. Like flare-ups from a disease, I have good days and bad days. I survive. I have learned a few things about survival.

As #MeToo has waned, other social movements have come and gone as well. BLM, COVID, Israel, Epstein. When one panic passes, another takes over, and more people go down. Rinse and repeat. It's normal now, as are groveling public apologies and expert, PR-vetted statements. But, as cancellation becomes more commonplace, so does the recovery from it. Except for OG cancellations. We the original cancelled, especially in small, sealed worlds like advertising, remain on the scoreboard. And no one wants to roll back a win for their team.

The saying goes, "Write what you know." Well, I know about punishment and survival and perseverance and understanding and guilt and anger and humor and what it's like to try to still be creative. Being creative was all that I knew before. Now I know three things: dealing with being cancelled; pretending to be a happy dad, husband, friend, and neighbor; and using my creativity to survive. And by survive, I mean survive. Like, not-go-to-the-roof survive.

In this book, as I run through some of my #MeToo experiences, I will attempt to put my cancellation in broader cultural contexts, which is kind of like throwing a piece of mangled driftwood into the ocean and then writing about the driftwood's "context." I'll tell you about the things I obsess about: mobs, online anxieties, cruelty in the digital age, and social media narcissism. I have a lot to say on those subjects. Finally, I'll talk about the things I crave, like grace, acceptance, forgiveness, and maybe rekindling a few lost friendships.

To some, I will come across as defensive and tone-deaf. Yes, I've spent a lot of time working through defensiveness, which is how fear and anger manifest. There is a plot turn coming later, though. Letting go of anger and fear is a much bigger part of my life than I ever thought it would be. Anger is uncomfortable to those who come near it. Anger makes people (at least the people I know) embarrassed, and they want to run away. Especially ad people. There is no place in the world of advertising for anything other than an air of success, whether it's true or not. Everyone out there is doing great and killing it. If you're angry, you'll spill your rosé.

As for the tone-deaf part, I've noticed the phrase is often used in a derogatory way to dismiss points of view that don't align with the critique's view. But aren't we supposed to be having a conversation? #MeToo, and subsequent upheavals, always included calls for in-depth conversations. "We need to have a conversation." That's what this is; I'm attempting to add to the conversation. And I know #MeToo-ed men weren't supposed to be the added voices, but in other areas the problematic voices get heard to good effect. When we talk about gang violence, gang member voices are valued. Frank Abagnale was a notorious check-fraud perpetrator who became a valued FBI expert on fraud. Couldn't I help? Maybe?

I will also barrage you with a hodgepodge of content: quotes, experiences, books, interviews, podcasts, things I've read in publications like the *Free Press*, the *Daily Mail*, *The Atlantic*, and videos I've watched on TikTok. We are all the summation of our inputs, and I've been inputting. Oh, have I been inputting.

I'm also very aware that I will not, nor will I ever, be able to change some people's minds or alter perceptions of me. As Kat Rosenfield wrote about Alec Baldwin: "Actually, he's just about the most unsympathetic collection of things you can be in 2024: an old, white, rich, and famous man protesting his innocence."* I am aware that I am these things as well. Alec Baldwin also has a giant square head, just like me. But I do believe, I have to believe, that people grow. Maybe hard-held beliefs against others can soften over time.

One of the most compelling arguments for cancellation during social movements is that this will contribute to a collective greater good, and that an individual's plight doesn't matter in the face of that. As Lindy West wrote in her book, *The Witches Are Coming*, "This moment in history is about more than individual interactions between individual people." But that's easy to say when you aren't the individual in question. This book is one individual making sense of that larger moment.

This perspective should also help answer the questions of "Why now? Isn't that over?" Well, yes and no. The hype around #MeToo has died down; cancellations have not. The appetite for inflicting reputational damage is alive and well and coming to a person near you. Or you.

The greater the distance I have from that first day, the more I realize that utilizing the creative parts of my brain is what has kept me going. It's an extremely self-serving cliché among ad creatives

* As of this writing, Baldwin was acquitted of all charges relating to the accidental shooting of Halyna Hutchins. Maybe he's unsympathetic, but he's also rich, powerful, and famous. Hannah Gutierrez-Reed, the armorer on set, wasn't so lucky. She got eighteen months. Baldwin walked. Maybe I shouldn't have brought up any of this.

to say creativity is at the core of who you are, but maybe it actually is true. Being cancelled is the toughest creative brief I've ever gotten; my core is working hard on this one.

Later on, I'll get heavy about self-perception and the "what-is-it all-about" questions. What was this all for? It can't just be, as Freddie deBoer, one of my favorite writers, said, "motivated by (occasionally understandable) anger at how the moral fashion of a few thousand overeducated and overcaffeinated Democrats with Slack accounts bent the entire worlds of journalism, academia, and the creative arts out of shape, the heterodox thing has targets but no goals."[4] Some people who got cancelled veered right and abandoned their old selves; some put their heads down and kept working as if nothing happened. I allowed guilt and shame and sadness to overwhelm me and took to writing as a way to see light. To each his own.

Finally, I've allowed myself a sense of humor. I've tried not to let either heaviness or humor take over and get annoying. I want you to enjoy reading this. A lot of therapy, spiritual exploration, and some insanely powerful psychedelic experiences got you and me here, but writing has been the best thing. I do believe that creativity can *save.*

That's what this book is: an attempt to use creativity to save some of myself.

Sorry

You're on a list
Sorry, but you're at the top of the list
I'll try to protect you, but I have to protect the company
You'll be OK
No one takes this seriously
Don't freak out
Just stay quiet

Don't worry, we'll handle it
Everyone here loves you
You didn't do anything wrong
Everybody knows that

Stay silent
Don't say anything
Don't do anything
Let HR handle it
Anything you say may explode in your face
We're trying to help you

Don't worry
Let the lawyers handle it
Let PR handle it
We're trying to help you

We have to investigate you, don't worry
It's a way out. Don't worry
You have to understand, it's complicated
Don't worry

We found things in your emails
We can't show you
We can't tell you what they are
But we found things in your emails

We asked people for complaints about you
We had to ask people for complaints
We had to
There were complaints about you

We can't tell you what they are
We can't tell you who made them
We have to protect the people who made them from retaliation
Anyone could retaliate
We have to protect them

You're fired

Go find another career
Go on a vacation
Go to the gym
Get in shape
This could be great for you

Don't worry, we'll have a great second act together
Just sign this first
Don't worry, we'll work together again.
Just sign this piece of paper

We found proof you slept with people
No, we won't show it to you
OK, maybe you didn't sleep with anybody
OK, maybe we believe you
Just sign this piece of paper

It's not his turn to speak
Men need to listen
He needs to shut up
He needs to tell us what he's done
His silence means he's hiding something
If he defends himself he's guilty
If he's silent it means he's guilty

He said everything he ever did was all consensual
That's hilarious
With power there is no consent
No one wants to hear his pain

His pain doesn't matter
Women everywhere have been in pain
For decades
For centuries
Forever
By comparison his pain is nothing

He should never be allowed to walk into an agency again
He should just go away

Don't sue, you will lose
Defamation is almost impossible to prove
Don't sue, companies never forget
You'll never get hired again

He brought up his kids
How dare he talk about his kids
It's disgusting that he would bring up his kids in this moment
He is not the victim here

He should just go away
Find another career
Go work at Starbucks
Go work at Walmart

We are writing another article about you
And another
You get compared to Harvey Weinstein
We have to compare you to Harvey Weinstein
It gets clicks
I'm sorry, you get clicks
We need to get clicks, and you get clicks

Everyone knows it's bullshit
A lot of people love you
You have more support than you realize
The pendulum will swing back

It's bad out there
Everyone is under pressure
No way could we hire you
You should start your own agency
I feel for you

Are you OK?
You should take medication
Everyone misses you
You will be back

No one misses him
Everyone has moved on
No one remembers him
There is no path back

We have a plan
We'll get people to talk about healing
We'll get people to come together

I'm sorry

No one is interested
We tried talking to people
No one is interested

I'm sorry

Come speak
Everyone will love you
Come speak

I'm sorry
We shouldn't have let you speak

I'm sorry

We should start a company together
Let's talk about it
Later

You should work on my brand
You should start your own company
You should start a brand
You should start
You should

You have your kids
You have your life
You should be happy
You should be grateful

I'm sorry, someone is angry
We have to listen to them
We can't work with you

I'm sorry

I'm so sorry

Cancelled

A man's life is his work; his work is his life.

—Jackson Pollock

"I'm sorry." I hear "I'm sorry" *all the time.* The pity hurts. Knowing that I need the pity hurts. And getting kicked out of your tribe hurts. It really *hurts*. Advertising was my tribe. I built decades' worth of friendships, relationships, acquaintances.

In his book, *The New Puritans*, Andrew Doyle compares woke culture to historically strict religious societies:

> Cancel culture typically takes the form of humiliation through online censure and direct contact with the targets, employers, in order to deprive them of their livelihoods. Through social media, irreparable reputational damage can be inflicted even when there is no secure evidence for the accusations. Not only can this result in dismissal, but it can impede future employment prospects. Often the reactions are immensely disproportionate to the slight and the intentions of the transgressor are regarded as irrelevant. Practitioners of cancel culture deny it exists, and are often reframed as "holding the powerful to account.[5]

Yeah, that.

That's what hurt most about being fired. I loved Droga5, but it is the loss of the entire ecosystem of my career that really hurts. Advertising is *all* I know how to do. If the apocalypse ever breaks out, I would be the one to fling myself at the zombie horde so everyone else can get to the chopper. First, because I'm fat and slow and they would take a while to eat me, and second, because in a postapocalyptic world I won't have a role. Very, very few fortified settlements will need pithy taglines.

MeToo: What about the women you hurt? Shouldn't you talk about that first? Shouldn't that be the worst part of your guilt?

Ted: I'll say this again and again, because it's hard for anyone—including myself—to make sense of: Any and all accusations against me were anonymous. I don't know who I hurt or what they claimed I did, so you'll excuse me for being unable to devote an endless amount of energy to what no one will tell me.

MeToo: You should. That's the point of this whole thing.

Ted: I hear you. We will get back to that, I promise.

I worked for twenty-five years across Asia, Australia, Europe, South America, and North America. I've lived full-time in Singapore, New York, Buenos Aires, and Sydney. I knew *thousands* of people in advertising and related businesses and loved seeing them wherever I went.

You can spend a lifetime building friendships, building status, earning seniority and pretty much your entire sense of identity, only to have banishment yank it all away. I lost my job, all connection to the agency I helped build from the ground up, all speaking engagements, all judging positions. (I was set to be chair of the Titanium Lions the year I was fired. That's *the* plum award-show judging assignment.) I resigned my The One Club board seat. I *loved* The One Club, maybe even more than I loved Droga5. I went from being invited to *everything* to being invited to *nothing*, overnight.

Over the course of a career, layer upon layer of one's identity is formed, settling into sediment bands like those in geological formations. They accrue over years of achievement after achievement, creating the entire mountain that is you. For some (me especially), your persona is inseparable from your life's work. It's how you relate to others, it's literally who you are.

That identity has a symbiotic relationship to your community: you reaffirm it, it reaffirms you. You might rise and fall in stature, but usually such ups and downs happen gradually: a new job, a failed relationship, a club you join, the things that can slowly build up or chip away at your sense of self. Getting cancelled is that sense of self being hit with a bunker-busting bomb. It blasts apart those years of sediment; the rock layers don't stand a chance. Nothing is left. The following quote from "The Status Game: Male, Grandiose, Humiliated," in *Quillette:*

> If life is a status game, what happens when all our status is taken from us? What happens when we're made to feel like nothing, again and again and again? Humiliation can be seen as the opposite of status, the hell to its heaven. Like status, humiliation comes from other people. Like status, it involves their judgement of our place in the social rankings. Like status, the higher they sit in the rankings, and the more of them there are, the more powerful their judgement. And, like status, it matters. Humiliation has been described by researchers as "the nuclear bomb of the emotions" and has been shown to cause major depressions, suicidal states, psychosis, extreme rage, and severe anxiety, "including one's characteristic of post-traumatic stress disorder.[6]

The lack of ability to earn money is the first, worst impact. Your job is gone, and all immediate prospects to get a new job can disappear, too. It gets bleak. Almost everyone who's been cancelled makes far less money than they did before.

Friendships are a mixed bag, but a lot of them go. The friendships that were based on your status go quickly. People who saw you as money, like the old cartoon wolves that saw people as huge chicken dinners, are gone in a snap. People who thought your job title was cool fade away next. I never realized how many close friends were only close because my title made them look cool by hanging out with me.

The friends who stick around? Louis CK* said, "These are the times you realize who your true friends are, and then you look at them and say 'Ugh, you people?'" But shit, man, those *are* your real friends. The ones who hear you cry, the ones who like you even when you're being mopey. The ones who answer the phone when you call too many times.

And life doesn't stop. All the normal problems of life continue. Family illness, mortgage issues, a pipe leak, your kid has trouble in school, your house has termites. Everything keeps barreling along, in the very hard way life does. Now add a rich, creamy layer of perpetual shame, a thick slab of guilt, a swirl of loneliness, and top it with the fruit of financial terror, and you've got yourself quite a cake.

The future becomes murky. Who you thought you were, the path you thought you were on, all gone. Blank.

---

* Yeah, I'll quote him. Hate what he did, but you can't deny he's very intelligent and a great stand-up comedian. I'll quote more than a few comedians, because I truly believe they need to be heard. What more powerful way is there to challenge a belief than through humor? And Louis CK? This man was my Yoda when he talked about dating, marriage, and raising kids. Furthermore, his work ethic is incredible. He writes a new hour of stand-up every year, in a business where comedians keep the same routine for years (cough, Jerry Seinfeld, cough). His podcast ruminations on cancellation have gotten me through some bad nights.

Nicholas Christakis is a professor of Social and Natural Science at Yale. He became nationally famous during a dust-up in which students screamed at him for hours in a courtyard because his wife had written an email suggesting that they, the students, should be able to choose their own Halloween costumes, however offensive. The students vehemently disagreed, instead preferring bans and punishments for the threats to their safety that Halloween-costumes cause. Since then, he has written a lot about cancel culture, and this, from "Mobs, Scapegoats, and Courage" in the *Free Press* really rang true for me:

> It is no small thing to deprive an adult of a livelihood. To take someone's job away. If you're a writer or a reporter and you've been run out of the profession, for example, that's devastating. Your whole life has been devoted to this profession. And so not only do you lose your income, but you lose a lot of your identity. This is not a trivial sanction. Yes, we didn't burn you at the stake. That's true. But we did something very bad to you. We put a scarlet letter on you and we took away your job, and your friends were afraid to associate with you. These are devastating social sanctions, not to be trifled with. I have spoken, over the last ten years, to many people who have been the objects of these types of inquisitions, for lack of a better word. And I know of at least eight cases of people who seriously considered suicide because of the social ostracism.[7]

I mean, fuck, does anyone who *hasn't* been cancelled get it? Is there any way to explain to the average person what this feels like? It's so *lonely.* You become extremely conscious that you're the whiney asshole whose traumatic thoughts will never stop repeating themselves in your head, and so you stop yourself from bothering others about it. But they're there, all the time.

"Don't worry," friends say, "the pendulum will swing back." That fucking pendulum everyone brings up. "It swung too far, it will swing back soon." As if my life is something as banal and forecastable as interest rates or cold fronts. Anyone who talks pendulum doesn't come *close* to understanding the situation.

The following sections are paraphrased from Jonathan Rauch at The Brookings Institute in "How to Tell If You're Being Cancelled" in *Reason* magazine.[8] It consists of six parts; I've changed the order a bit:

1. **Punitiveness:** Are people denouncing you to your employer, your professional groups, or your social connections? Are you being blacklisted from jobs and social opportunities? Does what is being said to or about you have the goal—or foreseeable effect—of jeopardizing your livelihood or isolating you socially?

Um, yeah. I'm totally blackballed. People tell me to my face there's no way they would risk hiring me for fear of being attacked. In a few instances covered in this book, you'll see that when it's discovered I am working for a company, employees who've never met me lose it and demand I be removed immediately.

2. **Deplatforming**: Are campaigners attempting to prevent you from publishing your work, giving speeches, or attending meetings? Are they claiming that allowing you to be heard is violence against them or makes them unsafe?

I used to give speeches and write articles all the time. After I was fired, I was rarely invited to do anything again—and when I was, it just made things worse every time. Just popping my head up generated a slew of anti-Ted posts and rumblings.

3. **Organization**: Does criticism appear to be organized and targeted? Are the organizers recruiting others to pile on? Are you being swarmed and brigaded? Are people hunting through your work and scouring social media to find ammunition to use against you?

I'd argue that Diet Madison Avenue, the anonymous Instagram account, was very well-organized, as well as Fishbowl, the app where people talk about each other. Like clockwork, a handful of the same people, anonymous except for their titles, would instantly pop up and attack anyone defending me or not shit-talking me hard enough. Furthermore, journalists dug deep into my past and tried to find anything they could use against me. I know this because two of them told me so to my face.

4. **Secondary Boycotts**: Is there an explicit or implicit threat that people who support you will get the same punitive treatment that you are receiving? Are people putting pressure on employers and professional colleagues to fire you or stop associating with you? Do people who defend you, or criticize the campaign against you, have to fear adverse consequences?

Yes, yes, yes, and yes. One former friend told me that, just because she was my friend, she was being attacked online for her association with me. Surprise, she's not my friend anymore.

5. **Moral Grandstanding**: Is the tone of the discourse ad hominem, repetitive, ritualistic, posturing, accusatory, outraged? Are people flattening distinctions, demonizing you, slinging inflammatory labels, and engaging in moral one-upmanship? Are people ignoring what you actually say—talking about, but not to, you?

I mean, of course. Read anything about anyone cancelled these days and you'll see moral posturing. One woman posted about a meeting with me and completely misrepresented the entire encounter. She also added, narcissistically, that I had been hitting on her (I most definitely had not). Pretty gross thing to make up about a man who's been MeToo-ed.

Furthermore, the outrage and cancellation often come from those who have either committed offenses that are much worse than I imagine I have, or the coworkers and continued allies of said people. This makes my head explode, except that when I think about it, it doesn't. Everyone is out for themselves all the time. Especially in the advertising world.

6. **Truthiness**: Are the things being said about you inaccurate? Do the people saying them not even seem to care about their veracity? Do they feel at liberty to distort your words, ignore corrections, and make false accusations?

Diet Madison Avenue tried to stick a knife in my heart with "inaccuracies" (otherwise known as "lies.") and even more insidiously had a spy follow me around in my office and report on things I said, then posted them along with mocking comments. It was a nightmare.

Rauch sums his definition of cancellation up in one chilling sentence: "The point is to make the errant suffer."

I understand that most people just want to lead quiet lives. They want to do their jobs, pay their rent or mortgage, fall in love, raise their kids, play video games, and die in their beds surrounded by family. *No one* wants to be dragged into the hateful messes that cancel culture creates, so people avoid being involved as much as possible. No one needs this. No one wants this. People kill themselves over this shit. Cancel culture is cruel, sadistic, and inhumane, and it personifies the worst tendencies of human beings and their worst primal urges.

I'll end with this quote from Taylor Swift in a *Vogue* article. Because even if you hate me, it's Taylor Swift and you have to listen to her:

> When you say someone is cancelled it's not a TV show. It's a human being. You're sending mass amounts of messaging to this person to either shut up, disappear, or it could also be perceived as "kill yourself."[9]

You can buy and live in the most beautiful
and expensive house in the world,
but you're still trapped in your head at night.
—Darby Hudson (S3 E1)

The McMann Fiasco

"Pooh" he whispered.
"Yes, Piglet?"
"Nothing," said Piglet, taking Pooh's paw.
"I just wanted to be sure of you."

—FROM *WINNIE-THE-POOH*, BY A.A. MILNE

These lovely sentences were texted to me by Lila Dolion, right after I was fired in 2018. Lila was then the CEO of McMann & Tate,* a large ad agency. This agency was originally part of what some called the "creative revolution" of the '60s.

I reached out to Lila after being fired. I reached out to dozens of people, looking for hope, looking for some sort of sustenance, something, anything. Lila was very kind to respond.

We chatted over the phone and through text for a few weeks. She offered advice, listened to me complain, and was genuinely empathetic. Lila had been an executive muckety-muck at a large food brand and my client a couple years prior. She was supportive

* Names have been changed. McMann & Tate was the agency in *Bewitched*, so it seemed funny to me to use here. And no, it's not McCann.

of Droga5 and pushed for good work. But not too hard, as pushing hard at her old company was not the best career move, and above all Lila was a survivor. She was just settling into her role at McMann and was very optimistic.

It was also, frankly, thrilling to have a high-profile woman in my corner. A woman who was part of Time's Up Advertising, a group that was formed at the height of #MeToo to address harassment issues and the struggles of women in advertising and had pretty much every high-ranking female lining up to join. It was a group I didn't think I had anything to fear from, as many of my friends and acquaintances were on it. People like Susan Credle, who took me out to dinner twice after I was fired, listened to me, and even cried with me. And Colleen DeCourcy, then the Worldwide CCO of Wieden, who came over to our house, hugged me, and told me she would do anything she could to help. Yes, it was thrilling to have such people listening and understanding.

Lila wrote:

> Hey you.
>
> Winding my way to ATL and reflecting on the last week or so. Exhausting & exhilarating. And you'd fall into the latter.
>
> Loved seeing your smile again. I have no concept of your journey til now but that wry smile was back. And all seems possible from there.
>
> I, along with so many of your fans, am right here. Whenever you need an ear, shoulder, half-wit brain, swift kick in the ass or a full-on hug (no half hugs please).
>
> Just shout.
>
> Keep on keeping on. I know there's more path to go. But you will journey it for sure. Xx

Exhilarating. I had hope.

Even more hope when Bo Childers, my friend who was the worldwide CCO of McMann, called and asked for help with pitching a car account. A car account! The account that made McMann famous! And now here was a chance to help that brand to return to the agency that sparked a revolution advertising cars and buses. Amazing. Of course, I said yes.

And then it just got worse.

I was invited up to the office to meet with the team and have a kickoff meeting for the pitch. Bo graciously showed me around.

After that we went to the main conference room, where a whole bunch of executives, the New York president, and Lila had assembled.

And two young women.

Immediately I knew I had made a huge mistake. These two women, with relatively junior titles, looked at me as though I were an evil clown who had just walked into the room covered in blood and hair. They were frozen. They didn't say anything. But they were *seething* and seemed to be trying not to show it because of the high-powered company they were in. Dammit. I should have known better.

Afterward, Bo and I met up in a coffee shop over the next couple of weeks. He would bring the team's work for the pitch, and I would help sort through it, finding the best ideas, shaping the approach, and seeing what needed to be sorted out further. It was fun, Bo was a good collaborator, and I was happy to help creative direct again. The best bit was that he started throwing out long-term scenarios. Would I like to run Dallas? Would I be interested in Torchfire NY, a new branch of a recently-acquired agency that had just opened up? I was so grateful that these conversations were even happening. Lila echoed them, if more vaguely, but definitely hinted that we had a good future together.

After a few meetings like this, Bo had me meet up with his New York creative director on the pitch, Ellen. And it was clear from the very beginning Ellen was not happy about working with me. We had met in the past and been friendly, but now I was TED ROYER, the clown covered in blood and hair, and Ellen was *just barely* tolerating me.

I tried my best with Ellen. I talked with her at length about my experience and listened to hers. She, like so many women, had some pretty harrowing life experiences to share, and I was honored to hear them. But workwise, it was clear she resented my involvement and point of view on creative matters. Bo was there to have final say, but his style was to avoid conflict, and I gathered that things behind the scenes were getting political.

Bo and I continued to talk, but we both agreed I wouldn't go to the agency anymore. One meeting was held in Lila's apartment. I remember it well for two reasons. I was the first to arrive and Lila and I chatted. She is a pleasant enough small-talker, but I often manage to say the wrong thing. Like, a lot of the time. This case was no different.

Me (looking around)**:** These corporate apartments are always decorated so blandly.
Lila: I decorated this place myself.
Me (checking to see if the window opens so I can jump)**:** Oh.

The second thing that happened at the meeting was weird, and sad. It was nothing to do with the people in the group, who were smart and focused and fine enough to work with. It was *me*. I was off. I was quiet. I was weirdly *guilty*. Not #MeToo guilty—I had had that feeling for months. This was a new guilt. After the talks with Lila and Bo about making this my next job, I felt like I was . . . I was cheating. *Oh my god*, I thought, *I'm cheating on Droga5*.

Eleven years and Droga5 had become so ingrained in my mind that working for another agency felt like I was betraying them. It didn't matter that they had thrown me out; I felt deep disloyalty for working this closely with another agency. It is a weird feeling that has stayed with me through every pitch and client meeting I've had since. Even today. A feeling I've heard about from people who've gotten a divorce and never gotten over their ex, even after being remarried for years.

And then shit began to rise high in the air and arc toward the fan.

First, both Bo and Lila told me that there were rumblings in the agency about me working there, but they had it under control. Lila talked to people. Bo talked to people. They said it was going to be fine.

Then the pitch came. The pitch, for those who don't know, is when different agencies compete for the brand's account by presenting a strategy, creative work, and their overall thought-out approach as to how they will handle the brand. On sites like AgencySpy and Fishbowl, chatter started to get intense about me and my involvement in the pitch. Accusations were random and fanciful. People were saying I had killed everyone's ideas but my own. What? How would that even be possible? Then they said that I had flown to Japan for the final pitch and ruined the presentation. I wished I had gone, that would have been cool. But no, I did not go. The McMann team said it went well.

After the pitch Lila sent me this:

Ted,
You are a star.
You were there every step of the way with Bo.
That was invaluable.
And you made our work BETTER.
We're massively sleep deprived. But ever thankful.
Dinner soon. xx

I think what pushed the situation over the edge was . . . McMann lost the pitch. Unbeknownst to me, they had pitched a commitment to setting up an entirely new agency to service the account. McMann wouldn't handle the account. A new entity would. The agency that made the car brand famous wouldn't be handling the car brand's account? What an entirely bizarre choice, one that threw away an extremely strong home-court advantage.

Of course, I wasn't there for these discussions, and I do not know exactly why these decisions were made, and I'm sure if you asked the team, they'd have all sorts of reasons about why they did what they did. Setting up side-agencies was a common practice for McMann, with one being created to handle a beverage brand. Ad agencies *love* to do whatever seems modern and cool, and a while ago setting up bespoke agencies for clients was hot. The clients felt super special, and the agencies created the illusion their network was growing. Of course, when they lost the business, that agency they set up just for that one account folded, thus showing the glaringly obvious fatal flaw in the "one agency, one client" strategy. But really, it was just sad. This was McMann and its car, a famous partnership McMann admitting it wasn't going to handle this car account was like saying The Beatles wouldn't be writing the lyrics for their next album.

Then everything really got worse.

After the loss, the press jumped. An evil clown carrying a baby's head had been set loose inside McMann. How could management have endangered everyone on staff with my presence like that? How could Lila Dolion work with a monster covered in blood and hair? How could they have endangered women like that?

Bo was apologetic to me, but distant. He said he had been advised not to say anything to anyone, which was a stance that, if you know him, is very Bo-approved. Avoid conflict. Stay alive. Lila? I texted Lila, who was going through a press bloodbath. It shook her. Or so I was told by others, because she completely stopped communicating with me.

I still needed an ear, a shoulder, a half-wit brain, a swift kick in the ass, or a full-on hug (no half hugs please). I needed all of that. Because any chance of recovering myself or recovering my career was swiftly lost with this fresh round of press lashings.

Lila said to the press, "If I had known then what I know now, I would have never hired him." Which is a startlingly disingenuous thing to say. It implies that she learned something new and insidious about me, which she did not. What it *also* could possibly mean is, "If I had known how mad you all would get, I never would have hired him." The wording is sneaky, crafty, and obviously lawyer-approved.

Winning the account may have helped, but the McMann fiasco proved that Ted Royer was well and truly unhireable. Anyone previously willing to take the risk would definitely not do so now. Lila survived. Bo survived. Our friendships did not.

Pooh?
Pooh? Are you there?
(Reaches for paw, finds nothing.)
Pooh?
Pooh?

A Conversation With MeToo

MeToo: Oh please.
Ted: What?
MeToo: Waaah.
Ted: Oh. You think I'm just whining?
MeToo: You are just whining.
Ted: Wow. I'm in so much pain, I'm in the middle of pouring out my most terrifying, sad thoughts and moments, and you respond with "waaah."
MeToo: Dude, no one wants to hear your pain. Fuck off.
Ted: Yeah, I've heard that a lot. From some people I thought were close.
MeToo: Well, it's true. Women have been in pain for years. Decades, centuries. The last thing we want to hear is some old (and white) guy whining about his pain.
Ted: So, I have to be judged against the pain of *all* women?
MeToo: Get over yourself. This is a moment for women.
Ted: But you are comparing me and whatever I have done to what's happened to all women. You're using every woman's pain everywhere to justify piling their collective pain on me.

MeToo: It's time for men to start paying. Tag, you're it. Deal with it.
Ted: I am dealing with it. I'm trying to deal with it. But this feels like I've been given a life sentence for an entire cause, not for what I've done.
MeToo: It's not only you, men everywhere are finally getting called out.
Ted: OK, fair enough, but can I be treated as an individual and be called out on behalf of the people I actually hurt, without taking on some vague, massive generalized anger?
MeToo: Fine. What did you *actually* do?
Ted: I'm not sure.
MeToo: Bullshit.
Ted: No, I'm *actually* not sure. I was accused online of stuff that I didn't do. "Grooming" women for years, forcing people to sign NDAs. Assaulting a woman in a hallway. I never did any of that, ever. I never would assault anyone, ever. I've never "groomed" anyone. I've never asked anyone to sign an NDA regarding anything other than confidential work or done anything else in an attempt to silence or dispute anyone.
MeToo: Now you're just being defensive.
Ted: Because I'm defending myself!
MeToo: Don't raise your voice. This is not the time for your anger. Lindy West wrote: "Not only are women expected to weather sexual violence, workplace discrimination, institutional subordination, the expectation of free domestic labor, the blame for our own victimization, and all the subtler, individual cuts that undermine us daily, we are not even allowed to be angry about it."[10] This is the time *we* get to be angry, not you.
Ted (quieter): OK. But I am being defensive because I am defending myself. Whenever I've written anything denying those accusations, I'm told I'm being defensive. What

kind of movement refuses to consider any defense at all? I'm dying here; I have to defend myself.
MeToo: Defensiveness is not what we need right now. Your defensiveness is not helpful.
Ted: When Droga5 fired me, I was told that two women had complained. But they didn't, wouldn't, tell me who the women were or what they had accused me of doing.
MeToo: Bullshit. You know.
Ted: No, I don't know. I have a guess, but I don't know for sure so I can't make assumptions—which I say in deference to any woman I worked with. I heard a rumor that I'd given an "inappropriate hug." I've never given a creepy hug in my entire life.
MeToo: No one is buying that.
Ted: I don't care if you buy it, it's the truth. They said that they had real dirt on me, which scared the shit out of me. Their lawyer even said they had "proof" that I'd slept with employees. I never had sex with anybody. At the time, I thought this was the line not to cross. Smart, huh?
MeToo: You were a flirt. You hit on women. You were known for this.
Ted: Yes. That is true. And that wasn't life-destroying stuff until a few years ago. Coming up in advertising, it seemed like everyone was doing something, and everyone who was fooling around was doing it by their own choice.
MeToo: Not everyone. And that needed to stop.
Ted: Maybe so. But people should be allowed to change with the times, no?
MeToo: Or the times should change people, and for that to be done quickly and effectively the consequences need to be swift and severe.
Ted: And random, apparently.
MeToo: Not random; they had enough to fire you.

Ted: Apparently they did.
MeToo: Apparently nothing. They did, right?
Ted: I guess so. But they also pressured me. And there are people who committed far worse than me still out there in the industry, still standing on stages and accepting awards, still having affairs.
MeToo: There are people out there committing crimes or other reprehensible acts, but once someone is caught, you can't believe we should let them go because others are still doing the same?
Ted: We also supposedly have a balanced justice system where someone does the appropriate time to pay their debt. Mine seems like a life sentence.
MeToo: No one should shed a single tear for you. You're a privileged asshole who got caught and fired. The world needs to spend its emotional energy anywhere else than on you.
Ted: Certainly feels that way. But I am a human being having a human experience. A human being who never intended harm to anyone.
MeToo: So, if you're so innocent, why didn't you fight back? Why didn't you sue?
Ted: That's so easy for people to say. "Why didn't you sue?"
MeToo: If you're so innocent, why didn't you?
Ted: Many reasons.
MeToo: Go on.
Ted: OK, here we go. I didn't sue Diet Madison Avenue because I kept getting legal advice that I wouldn't win. Defamation is very hard to prove. I was told the process would last years and cost hundreds of thousands. I was scared for my dwindling finances and my family's future, and for my mental health. Lawsuits are (to me) terrifying and mentally draining. Some people love them, but the year

I went through with lawyers just to deal with my firing was too painful to extend. Also, they were anonymous and still are. Still hiding.

MeToo: Other people have sued and seemed to find success.

Ted: Name one person who did.

MeToo: Johnny Depp.

Ted: That was four years later. The culture had shifted. That's why I'm writing about this now and not in 2018. My window to sue was at the height of MeToo, which brings me to my second point: If I sued, it would cement my position as an enemy, an enemy of the culture, an enemy of the movement. And I couldn't face that either. I don't think I'm a monster, and I don't want to fight. I *really* don't want to fight against this movement. Women feeling safe? Of course I don't want to fight against that. But that's what it felt like I would be fighting against.

MeToo: So why not sue Droga5, if you're so clean?

Ted: Because I wasn't clean. They had twelve years of reckless, casual email jokes. Twelve years of comments. Twelve years of GChats. When you take a GChat out of context and put it in the *New York Times* it gains a whole new level of power, power to destroy. Bill Burr does a whole great bit about it.* And they told me they had proof. They had a

* Burr: "No means no," that's another one. "No means no." It's like, no, it doesn't. All right? [laughter] Look, "*No!*" means no. "*No!*" That means *no,* all right? But [in flirty voice] "No, stop it, what are you doing? Oh, my God, you're being so bad. Stop it! No!" Yeah, that's not a fucking no! That means, "I wanna do it, but I'm afraid you're gonna judge me, so I'm just gonna make it look like it was your idea, so you don't figure out that I've already performed this act with forty other fucking people." Right? [laughter] But then, then you go to court and you get a bad reading. Some guy's reading it. [in serious voice] "Ah, Your Honor, she said, 'No, stop it. What are you doing? You're being so bad.'" [laughter] Yeah! And you're just sitting there like, "She didn't fucking say it like that! She didn't say it like that!"

terrifying ability to ruin me further and were not shy about telling me they would use it. I was afraid I would never work again on any level, so I curled up and stayed silent.

MeToo: So you were guilty.

Ted: Let's be fair: You could call almost anyone guilty if you dig enough. And they dug deep. I can't tell you the number of times people have sat across from me and said, "The same thing would happen to me if people dug up my emails." It's advertising. It's an industry that is (was) known for being reckless and creative. That was the beauty of it. We could be wild, and channel that wild energy into work. And create great work out of it. But in that environment, of course someone is going to say something stupid or offensive. A guy named Brett Craig was destroyed five years after the fact for a flippant email comment about race.[11]

MeToo: Was it racist? If it was, it sounds like he deserved it.

Ted: Sure, *everything* that sounds like a thoughtless act or comment deserves punitive consequences if you want to see it that way. You have to understand, until just a few years ago no one over the age of thirty thought we were living in a surveillance state. Only young people get it, they get that their comments and emails and of course tweets could be weaponized. I came of age in a world where being funny or sarcastic or flirty was *good*. I received nothing but positive feedback, as far as I could tell, for this attitude all the time. Every performance review I got was glowing. My creative department loved working for me, or so I was told. Then one day my Gen X flippancy became weaponized.

MeToo: You mean you faced the consequences of your actions.

Ted: If that's how you want to see it.

MeToo: That's how everyone sees it.

Ted: Yes, I know they do. But the world got different, and I was still living in the one of fifteen years ago, where saying and doing crazy stuff was OK. All I want now is the chance to live in the current one.

MeToo: "I was being an asshole and the world finally caught up to me." There, I fixed it for you.

Ted: I never thought I was an asshole. I never thought I was hurting anybody. Doesn't that count for something?

MeToo: Intention doesn't matter, only impact.

Ted: OK, I will have more to say on why that slogan is insane.

MeToo: Can't wait.

Ted: Can I say one more thing about the "Why didn't you sue" question? And it's the biggest thing.

MeToo: Sure.

Ted: I didn't sue Droga5 because I *loved* Droga5. I loved it. I loved walking the halls and talking to people. I loved when we all pulled together to make something. I loved the funny, smart, silly, creative people in that building.

MeToo: You do know that people sought out therapy because of their time at Droga5.

Ted: Yeah, I heard that. And I'm really sorry people felt that way. All I saw, and maybe all I chose to see, was the good, but wow, did the good seem great.

MeToo: What's your point?

Ted: My point is, I loved the people and that place too much to go to war with them. I couldn't sue; it would have broken my heart even more than it was already broken. It's like a divorce: the best way to handle a divorce that breaks your heart is to not fight it, but to go with it. Remove the resistance, so the other side has nothing to fight against. It's the only way to leave the door open for any reconciliation.

MeToo: You thought you would reconcile with Droga5?

Ted: Yes. I really thought I would. I was *so* invested in that place, I thought for sure they would call. For the first few weeks after being fired, I would often have the totally irrational thought: *Why is no one calling me about the work?* I was so wrapped up in it that my brain couldn't believe that we wouldn't at least see the work through. Then, for years, I kept thinking in the back of my mind, *they'll call soon.*
MeToo: That's pathetic. It's just an ad agency.
Ted: Not to me. It was so much more to me.
MeToo: Well, that's also your fault. You told your own employees when you fired them that "this place is not a family, it's a fast-moving company that has to make tough choices." Well, asshole, you got bitten by your own truth. They moved on.
Ted: I know.
MeToo: The point is, whether or not you meant to, you hurt people.
Ted: And is there no way to fix that?
MeToo: We are fixing it. By calling out the people who do it.
Ted: Selectively.
MeToo: Maybe, yes.
Ted: You can't, and don't, bring down everyone who deserves it. That would ruin too much.
MeToo: Yes, it's effective enough to make a few examples, punish them, so the rest of the herd stays in line.
Ted: Thank you for admitting that I'm a scapegoat.
MeToo: You are. You are a useful scapegoat.
Ted: Useful for being the target of anger and punishment. But I also like the word "useful" for what it can mean moving forward. I am writing this to *be* useful. We have to get beyond anger and pain. What would those next steps to move forward look like?

MeToo: How wonderful that you're here to show us all.

Ted: Stop it. I'm trying to help. It's the only way I seem to be able to stay sane.

MeToo: How exactly are you trying to help?

Ted: After being fired, I reached out and spoke to over one hundred of women. I have a much better understanding what they go through every day. I volunteered with an organization that goes into prisons and speaks with inmates on a humane, human level. It's amazing. I've also tried many times to work with different women's organizations. For one reason or another it's hard to get anything going. They either flat-out say no, thank you, or don't have money to produce anything, or, like some nonprofits, want to hold endless Zoom meetings and talk. But I'm still trying. I still have hope.

MeToo: OK, that sounds thin.

Ted: Yeah, the results are very thin, but I'm trying. I'm perhaps the safest person I can possibly be now, and I shut down sexual conversations about women, with them or about them. I'm that guy now.

MeToo: Big deal. You should have always been doing that.

Ted: Well, it's growth. What more can I do?

MeToo: Maybe go away and make space for someone else who isn't such damaged goods.

Ted: I am gone. But I'm not dead. And maybe I have more to contribute. I can do the work.

Sorta Kinda Doing the Work

Do the work. It's all we heard, throughout not only MeToo but every cancellation, for transgressions of all kinds. When you're cancelled, it's your job now to go away and *do the work*.

The problem is, no one knows exactly what the work is. What does that mean? Which work? Where? I'll do it! What are the hours? Do I have to wear a hat?

So, I went out and tried to do "the work." Results were varied, to say the least.

I wanted to make things right so badly that I looked for the work everywhere. But there is no official protocol, no handbook, no intensive, notary-certified, hoop-jumping program for completing the work. You have to kind of make the work up and hope the mob deems the work acceptable—which I'm not sure it ever has, at least not yet.

First, I wanted to hear from women. Women I knew. Women from advertising. Women I had never met. Women I'd flirted with. Women who I knew or suspected hated me. Any woman who might have been affected by my behavior, directly or indirectly. I made a goal to talk to one hundred women, a nice round number that would hopefully guarantee a huge range of perspectives. It was engaging, painful, enlightening, sometimes fun, and melancholy. Here are some highlights:

- I had very little idea how hard it is for women in advertising. What I thought was an enlightened industry was often performing its enlightenment, just as it performs its altruistic, "doing good," and "raising awareness" sides.*
- Women get hit on constantly. In advertising and everywhere else. Constantly.
- Asking a woman about her relationship, or whether she's in a relationship, is a form of harassment. It's not just invasive; it implies she's just an appendage to a man.
- "You flirted with me, and I thought it was fun."
- "You flirted with me, and I thought it crossed a line, even though I had to pretend it was fun."
- "You flirted with me, and it was both fun and crossing a line. It's complicated."
- Making out with someone who works for you sends a clear signal that you are a dangerous, unstable person. People do not want to work for dangerous, unstable people.
- If you write anything incriminating in a text, gchat, or email, you're an idiot.
- If any agency or company were to go through (insert person here)'s texts, gchats, and emails, that person wouldn't be cancelled, they'd be in jail.**
- Louis CK should be in jail.

---

* The advertising industry loves to say that it does "good." It also loves to say that it raises awareness of an issue. Both of these are often excuses to do work specifically aimed at winning awards. It works. The agency feels good, the client feels good, and the judges feel good. Advertising rarely checks to see how the rest of the world feels.

** It is hard to communicate how excruciating this is to hear, and I hear it all the time: "People did way worse than you and got away with it." Cool.

- Alyssa Milano does not speak for us.
- Alyssa Milano kind of speaks for us.
- There are two women out there, separate from anyone who may have complained about me, who hate my guts and say that I ruined their careers. I have never been told who they are or what they believe I did specifically, only that it was work-related and nonsexual. They have told others that they will never forgive me and also that they hope I die. This is nearly verbatim from one conversation.
- Men in advertising have always been assholes. During the Cannes advertising festival, one prominent CCO offered to pay a producer's rep if she would sleep with him. He was not joking. She laughed it off because she felt she couldn't react in any other way in order to avoid retaliation, and throughout the week he kept raising the offer. He is, of course, still working.
- This is all overblown and ridiculous.
- This is all very necessary and long overdue, and I need to accept my role in it.
- It's about time everyone became far more aware of what it's like being a woman in advertising. The awareness of being a woman is a permanent state, whereas the awareness of being a man is not. Women are forced to be aware of being a woman, from meetings to afterwork drinks to commutes home. One woman said, "You know when construction is being done on a building and they create those dark hallways under the scaffolding? I always check the corner mirrors they set up to see if a dangerous-looking man is around the corner." I asked, "What mirrors?" She responded, "Exactly."
- People have affairs. Affairs are fine and normal.
- People should never have affairs. Affairs are evil.

I could go on. The conversations were exhilarating and frightening. Did this count as work? It certainly felt like work.

I reached out to several women's organizations in advertising and offered to work for them for free. Some said no right away. Some were responsive but vague. A couple were enthusiastic, happy to have me work on ads and promotions for them. I wrote campaigns and film scripts for them. Very few got produced for lack of funds. One we did in AI and I really like it, but the organization got cold feet (because they had just been sued by men) and didn't run it. But still, this felt like good work.

Then I met a group that was deeply into the philosophy of restorative justice. Restorative justice, as defined by the *Oxford English Dictionary,* is "a system of criminal justice which focuses on the rehabilitation of offenders through reconciliation with victims and the community at large." A new group called The Harmony Initiative* (HI) was interested in applying restorative justice to the cases of men who had been MeToo-ed. They thought the ad industry would be a great place to focus, not only to raise the profile of the group, but also to find more funding for its mission.

Awesome. Sign me up. This is *the work.* I first talked with Anna, the lead therapist/healer/administrator. Anna was all business with me. In our initial exchanges, she came across as cold and clinical, resisting most attempts at levity. It soon became clear why. Anna and her team knew I had been a "name" in the industry, and that being able to dangle it would have some benefit for them. My involvement was a way for them to gain entry into the advertising community; on the other hand, using my name might not make the best first impression in the industry. They could use my knowledge to strategize an approach and help construct effective reach-out language, so long as they consistently, overtly positioned me as HE WHO HAS DONE HARM. That was my

* Not its real name, but created by ChatGPT on the first try.

role. I would be used in meeting scenarios as a proxy for other harm-doers, to facilitate healing conversations with those who had been harmed. Someone else on the team told me that very few men had signed up for this role, so I think they were thrilled to find someone who would. Furthermore, and most important to them, I was not to talk to anyone outside of the organization about HI or my involvement in it in any way. I was to remain silent; my name would be used only by them when and only when it was strategically useful to them.

Um . . . OK. I was just happy to be doing the work.

I joined Zoom calls to see HI in action. These calls were online meetings with dozens of participants, designed to bring the HI community together and hear from some prominent advocates and ostensible beneficiaries. I can only describe HI calls as similar to what I've read about military combat: long periods of boredom punctuated by moments of sheer terror. The boredom hit right out of the gate, in the endless land acknowledgments that came first on the agenda for each meeting. I timed it once: the land acknowledgments went on for seventeen minutes before the speakers were introduced.

The terror came later. In one session, we heard from a convicted child molester who had convinced himself that what he had done with an underage, preteen child had been love. His testimony was *riveting*. I'd never met someone guilty of such a thing or heard their perspective. He took accountability while clearly still reeling from his own actions. And as he did, my horror partially gave way to empathy. This man was clearly in agony, struggling with the crime he had committed. Maybe there really was something to the idea of restorative justice.

Then there was a personal call with three HI staff members: Hannah, Katie, a soft-spoken young woman who seemed gentle and empathetic, and Tom, a thirty-something male who was silent and stern. The call was frosty and formal, despite my attempt to make it loose and friendly (I have a weakness where I assume that everyone I work with is my friend). We talked about what we could do within the industry, what effective ideas or systems we could implement. I say "we" only to make the conversation sound somewhat logical. HI again, as always, went to great lengths to remind me repeatedly that we weren't a "we." I was in no way a part of HI, they said, I was HE WHO HAS DONE HARM. This end-all, be-all stance began to wear down my willingness to help. I began to see that HI was just as judgmental toward someone in my position as anyone else.

Wasn't it their mission to break down preconceived notions in order to see the human being in everyone? By their own definition, they were reconcilers. If they weren't willing to reconcile with me as a person who—again, by their own definition—deserved a chance to explore my past, how could they be open-minded in other encounters, when the issues could get way more intense, when angry and hurt people might get involved?

Then it got worse.

At one point, I was describing the ins-and-outs of the ad industry as I knew it, talking about people, coworkers, relationships, agency dynamics. And I said that agency atmospheres could sometimes get "bitchy."

I'm a man of a certain age. The word "bitchy" has never been a nice one. Bitch has always been a brutal one. Bitch-*y* wasn't as bad, but it wasn't good. It meant "mean," "backstabbing," or "political." But it didn't have the power that the folks at HI were about to ascribe it. Tom, the only other man on the call, sat up straight, leaned in, stopped everything.

"Ted, I'm going to have to stop you there and ask that you not use that word." Tom couldn't repeat the word, only refer to it.

"Which word, 'bitchy'?" Tom winced ever-so-slightly as I said it again.

"Yes. Don't say that word." Tom's tone was one of rising anger. He was feeling his moment.

"OK, sorry," I said.

But Tom wasn't done. "It's demeaning and misogynistic."

"Got it."

"Let's never use it again," Tom said, completely unnecessarily, bathing in the approving gaze of his coworkers.

"OK." I said, chastised.

"Now let's move on." Tom ordered.

Who was Tom to say *move on* after he had made this a bigger deal than it needed to be? For someone who hated misogyny and probably railed against toxic masculinity whenever he could, Tom was alpha-male-ing all over the place. And it was easy for him to play alpha male over HE WHO HAS DONE HARM. While facing a person in a cooperative, helpful, willing-to-please posture, Tom was throwing punches to prove his superior bona fides.

"Hey, everyone," I said, "I'm here really, really wanting to help, but if I'm going to be treated like a villain every time I make the slightest mistake, well, that doesn't seem to be in the spirit of restorativeness, does it?"

Katie, heretofore quiet, chimed in. "Did Tom's comment impact you as aggressive?"

"Yeah. It did."

Katie said, "I'm sure Tom meant it as helpful. Didn't you, Tom?"

With Katie arbitrating, Tom's alpha-light began to dim slightly. He responded with less volume. "Yes, I meant it as helpful."

"So," I went on, "Can we not chastise each other? I'll make mistakes and maybe you all will make mistakes, but this is kind of a partnership. We need each other and—"

Hannah, the most senior among us, broke in. "No. This is not a partnership. You in no way represent HI or have any say over this process or our decisions as an organization."

I responded, "I know. You've told me that a hundred times. But let's be clear, you're using my name to get to the ad industry. You'll be using my contacts. You'll be asking me to back-channel with the people I know. So, while I understand the formal structure you can't wait to remind me of, we kind of need each other, don't we?"

Hannah wasn't happy with this. I was not being a good HE WHO HAS DONE HARM. There were long pauses. Katie tried to reconcile everyone again. Tom had gone quiet. Hannah had gone quiet.

The meeting ended cordially with promises to work better together. HI was going to come back with a plan to reach out to the ad industry to outline for me my exact role in such outreach.

And nothing happened.

HI went quiet. Hannah, who had been my first contact there, stopped responding. I back channeled, as I'd agreed to, with a few prominent people. No one wanted to go anywhere near the project. #MeToo had moved on, and they had moved on with it. Katie, bless her heart, kept communicating with me long afterward. Weeks later, she explained to me that HI had attempted to contact several agencies to see if they wanted to discuss implementing restorative justice practices when faced with accusations or disputes, but that no one had been interested. I asked to see how they had reached out, what they wrote, etcetera. She said she couldn't show me any correspondence. We exchanged a few more emails, interesting ones about perpetrators, victims, and the potential to heal. I sent her articles about #MeToo. I probably annoyed her, wanting to defend myself and show how much gray area there was in all this. I can be a little exhausting for some on the subject, and I guess I exhausted Katie eventually, because she went silent, too.

So, no more doing the work there.

From the appearance of it, Louis CK did go away, for a while, but then he started doing stand-up appearances again, ignoring "the work" and just doing his work. He is playing Madison Square Garden again this year. He's back. After slapping Chris Rock on live national TV, Will Smith did some work. Apparently, his work consisted of traveling to India and then producing a video depicting how he *forgives himself.* After that, *Bad Boys 4* killed it in theaters. Excellent work-doing, Will.

Maybe whatever work you do isn't really the point. Maybe the point is to fuck off for a while. Maybe others want you to do work that reinforces their perceptions, and nothing more.

I don't know. But if anyone has a helpful idea about more work I can do, I'm available.

I Hate Advertising

I hate advertising.

I hate how ads use fear to convince you to buy something. Fear that you aren't cool. Fear that you're missing out. Fear of breath that smells bad. Fear of laundry that smells bad. Fear of not looking cool. Fear of not acting now. Fear of time. Fear of age. Fear of decay. Yes, that's what this world needs, more fear. Let's manufacture some with ads!

I hate how ads use your own narcissism to sell something to you. Every recent ad boils down to this message: "You, the consumer, are *amazing*. We know this, so we made our product to unlock the *amazing* inside of *you*." You aren't amazing, the product isn't amazing, and your life won't be more amazing when you buy it. Look around, on TV, on YouTube pre-roll ads, on social, on the subway, you will definitely see an ad telling you that *you are amazing* and we know it and you know it so let's unlock it together; give us your money! I hate the hypocrisy of an industry that claims to be "doing good" while clearly doing everything for money, awards, and recognition.

I hate the effort that the industry pours into trying to convince others (and ourselves) that we are somehow pure and good, and not total greed-heads.

I hate Super Bowl ads. "Hey here's an idea, let's convince a client to pay seven million dollars* to get as many celebrities as we can to spout dumb jokes in a complicated, ridiculous concept in the hopes of distracting enough people to rank it high on the *USA Today* Ad Meter." Super Bowl ads are horrible, representing the very least of the industry's creative potential, and the whole industry knows it. Yet everyone pretends that they are great. And average people pretend to like the ads. Or to hate them. Or to care at all. When nobody really cares. The Super Bowl is both sides, advertising and the public, showing contempt for each other while pretending to love each other.

I hate car ads. Everyone driving in a car ad has a stupid, smug look on their face while they drive whatever piece-of-shit car the ad is selling. No one looks like that when they drive. Smug Driving Face is a prerequisite of every car ad.

I hate ads with dancing. So many ads just show people dancing. Because TikTok has so much dancing, people say, "Oh, dancing is popular, let's do dancing." Dancing is not an idea. Dancing is the lack of an idea. Dancing is the idea you approve of when you're scared to do anything else.

I hate the award shows, those self-serving spectacles, the glitz, the pomp we create all to hand out awards for ads, things that people strive every day to ignore. Yes, I used to go to them, I used to pretend that I loved them. And I did love the attention. But inside I hated the spectacle and I hated myself. I hate that adults, grown adults, need awards. All the time. I hate that we give awards to adults. We crave awards, need them for validation. Watch Jim Carrey's 2016 Golden Globes speech.

I hate judging award shows. I hate the obvious politics, the bitterness, the killing of a rival's work out of spite and jealousy, and the behind-the-scenes horse trading. Oh wow, the horse trading.

* For a 30-second Super Bowl spot in 2025. If you're reading this later, it's definitely more expensive.

When one judge says to another, "I'll promote your piece of work if you promote my piece of work." It happens all the time, and it's gross and pathetic.

I hate that big agencies hire people whose sole purpose is to game award shows, knowing which categories are vulnerable, where they can best win, where to carpet-bomb a show with lots of entries, and how to time the entering of which pieces in different award shows for maximum results. It is a totally gamify-able system, and it's gamed all the time. I talked with one person who does this as his job, his only job, and listened to his submission strategies. I said, to his face, "You make me not want to be in this business." The comment bounced right off him like a bullet bounces off Superman as he kept right on proudly explaining his strategies.

I hate the clients. Smug, indifferent amateurs who say they want good work but just want to keep their jobs. I hate caring about brands *far more* than the people running them do. I hate having to pretend that their criticism is smart or valid, when it's really just fear. I hate dealing with their fear, the fear that gets in the way of making something good.

I hate the meetings. The endless fucking meetings that exist just so some disinterested manager can feel that they are "up to speed." The meetings about doing work instead of actually doing work. The meetings that are held just so someone can feel like their ass has been properly kissed. I talk to people who are on Zoom meetings all day long. Zoom meetings are not work, they aren't spaces to think, create, plan.

I hate the self-congratulation around the diversity initiatives, which are really just ways for agencies to cover their asses and avoid being accused of racism. So, they hire a bunch of people for their race, and their numbers look good. One global CCO actually said to me, "Send me any Black people you know, I'll hire them. Done." Do they do any special work to integrate these people? Do they train them? Do they do everything to ensure they succeed? In the words of a prominent Global Human Resources Director,

"Of course we don't." As far as I can see, only Wieden + Kennedy is truly following through with a real transformation. So much is empty show. I'm all for diversity; I'm not all for empty posturing and ass-covering. Also, of course both people quoted above are white. In the words of comedian Winston Hodges: "I think we should diversify every position, except the one that I hold. We should get more Black people in here except my job. Not my job."

I hate pitching. I hate having to scramble some work together and beg for business we don't really want so we can get a headline or some meager billing. I hate being told we have a budget of $2 million, only to hear, "Actually we have $1 million," and then, "Actually it's $500,000 and it's not agency of record, it's a project." Did you feel good lying to everybody? Great job. And I hate lying when I say, "We're so excited to work with the team," to the same team that has just put us through a dumb audition process and will probably fire us within a year.

I hate the way the business runs on whims. The whims of a client who will drop you. The whims of a boss who will hire someone just because of some random reason or intangible thing. The whims of some online comment that makes everybody's heads spin.

I *hate* banner ads. They pollute everything and *no one* ever clicks on them. A good, effective banner ad gets a 3 percent click rate. That means 3 percent of the people who see them at that moment click on them. Subtract clicking by accident and that number goes way down. Then subtract the number of people who clicked intentionally and then regret it by immediately leaving the site they were brought to and the number plummets further. Banner ads suck. They are the nadir of creativity and effectiveness.

I hate speeches by ad people. Every ad person who gives a speech pours on a thick, rich, noxious combination of braggadocio and humility wrapped around a desperate attempt to look cool and relevant. And often the stats or successes ad people mention in their speeches are outright lies. No one checks or challenges them.

Speaking of bragging and humility, I hate ad people on LinkedIn. If you believe LinkedIn, then every ad person is doing amazingly well, really killing it out there, and is incredibly *humbled* and *honored* to be doing whatever. Ad people have no idea what the word "humbled" actually means. You know what truly humbled people don't do? Brag on LinkedIn. LinkedIn is the Bonobo monkey tribe. The Bonobo monkeys masturbate themselves and each other in order to communicate and socialize. That's LinkedIn.

I hate, just hate, the way advertising instantly, automatically jumps on every social cause. In their mad dash to appear on the side of Good, ad people will sprint over to the "correct" side of any cause, rational thinking and consequences be damned. Yes, this includes #MeToo, which the industry immediately and wholeheartedly embraced. But also, every other cause. Because advertising feels guilty about the amount of money it makes in the name of capitalism and mass manipulation.

I hate it when someone in advertising struggles with the idea that they work in a capitalist system. I got news for you, Claire, if you work in advertising you aren't just a pawn in the capitalist system, you are a soldier fighting on the front lines of Capitalism with a capital C. You are a full-blown, blood-covered, armed-to-the-teeth warrior for that shit.*

---

* Jon Stewart on *The Daily Show*, July 8, 2024: "Why are we allowing ourselves to get worked up over whether giant multinational corporations are pro-gay or have traditional American values because corporations have but one value, shareholder value. That's all they have. That Budweiser horse that wants to restore our American spirit is owned by a Belgian-Brazilian beverage conglomerate. That Clydesdale's name is probably Jean-Luc Bolsanaro. Even the corporations you think are sincere, like Dove and their mutiyear commitment to body positivity, are owned by Unilever, also the owner of Axe Body Spray, and their decades-long commitment to fucking anything that moves. There is nothing corporations do that is not in service to their bottom line. . . . Let's let corporations live their truth, as the profit-seeking Patrick Bateman psychopaths that they are."

I hate cute taglines. You know, the ones with fake simplicity that sound like they are written so that imbeciles will get them? Baby-talk taglines, like "Do Travel Good" or "Be The Yeeahh."

I hate when someone in advertising tells me about a new job and then says, "Don't tell anybody." As if anybody gives a shit about your new GCD title, Simon.

I hate that ad people's highest aspiration used to be becoming movie directors, screenwriters, and artists. Now we can't wait to be considered "consultants."

I hate ad people. To my former advertising friends: as Douglas Murray said, "There are some times in your life when a flare goes up, and everybody can be seen precisely where they are standing." Thanks, I can see.

I Love Advertising

I love advertising.

I love seeing great ads. It gives me a real thrill to be stopped in my tracks by something creative and great.

I love that there is an industry comprising thousands of people who want to see great ideas live in the world. Not everybody in advertising does; many people just want to pay their mortgage and raise their kids, but there are many who wake up excited about bringing an idea to life.

I love seeing great craft at work. I love little creative details in ads you miss the first few times you see it. I love seeing thoughtful details that didn't have to be there but are. Like the Etsy 2024 ad that has a title card midway that reads, "Later, in France . . ." What a hilarious, silly detail.

I love when music elevates an idea. Music is half the battle sometimes. Mike Ladman should be the best-paid person in the business. He's a music producer who makes everything he works on so much better. When an ad moves you to tears, it's because of the music. Volkswagen's Pink Moon is a good ad made great by Nick Drake's "Pink Moon." And that is no fault of the creatives; that's a huge shout-out to their talent. They were smart enough to let the song do the talking.

I loved working late in an agency. I used to stay late at my office all the time. Before I had kids I would hang out, chatting, eating, drinking, playing video games. I loved the sense of place. I loved the sense of purpose. I loved the people there. And I loved that often being in an agency with fun, smart people felt better than being anywhere else.

I loved to see the setting sun bounce off the windows in Brooklyn, bathing the Droga5 office in golden afternoon light. It was gorgeous.

I love campaigns. I love when you find a repeatable device or formula that doesn't wear out its welcome. Like All-State's Mayhem. Or best of all, "This Is SportsCenter." I love the moment when I realize I'm seeing a new execution of a campaign I already know. I root for it. I hope the new execution lives up to the bar that was set before. And I love knowing that somewhere somebody was having a great time figuring out how to live up to it.

I love my clients. I love getting to know their fears and ambitions and truly getting to help them. I love the moments when we really talk about what the brand and company can be. I love hearing their hopes and goals and creating that shared sense of mission. I love knowing we rise and fall together. Nothing, and I mean *nothing* in advertising happens without a great, brave client.

I love company founders. They are almost always crazy driven. And when they start pounding the table, really going off about what they are trying to build, it's a rush to listen to, and an honor to be a part of. God bless crazy, driven founders.

I love brands. It's an honor to be able to inhabit a brand, get to know it, and speak for it. I love creating the living expression of a brand; what a thrill. I think we are incredibly lucky to live in a world surrounded by brands that want us to feel better, eat better, and live better. Sure, they want our money, but everyone throughout history has always had their money taken away by someone. At least brands can be held accountable. It's great to live in a world where we have brands dancing in front of us competing for our attention, dying to make us happier and healthier. Two hundred years ago, there was no Advil. *No Advil.* Now there's Advil and a dozen competitors all elbowing each other out of the way for a chance to get rid of my headache. That's *amazing*.

I love when an idea gets challenged, a real authentic challenge, and it survives to become better. Bring on the challenge. If my idea dies, so be it. If it lives, like a gladiator who survives an arena battle, it gets stronger.

I love staring at a wall, drinking coffee, and not knowing what we're going to do. And then someone says, "What if we . . ." And then a couple weeks later we are surrounded by a crew of dozens of amazing talented professionals bringing that "what if we . . ." moment to full, realized existence. How incredible.

I love award shows. I love that entire organizations exist to champion ideas and celebrate when those ideas thrive in the world. If you haven't seen an advertising award show, go to the award show called Cannes Lions' website; you will be astonished at the amazing ideas within. I was at another award show, The One Show, in 2016 sitting next to a guy from Silicon Valley. As one great idea after another was shown, he turned to me and said, "This is the best display of thinking I have ever seen." Fuck yeah, it was. Ad people, when they are on, can really bring it.

I love judging shows. I love the honest debate and the enthusiasm of smart professionals culling a body of work down to its very best set. I love how proud judges become of the body of work they will help the world to see. And how judges can bond so closely over the few days they are together. Some of my lifelong friendships began in judging rooms.

I love the camaraderie. I love the late nights. I loved the feeling we got when we cracked an idea together and everyone *knew* that was the one. The relief and elation when we just *knew*.

I love taglines. Many people say they are outdated or passé, but whatever. I love it when a brand's essence or idea is boiled down so succinctly to a few powerful words. The best ever is "Nike: Just Do It," but my favorite is still "Lexus: The Relentless Pursuit of Perfection." That line wraps the product, the brand's culture, and an ethos all into one powerful set of five words. Of course, they changed it to "The Pursuit of Perfection," which gutted it by removing the best word, and then they followed that with "Experience Amazing," which is cutesy and bland and could be used for literally any other product, not to mention any other car. "Hilton: Experience Amazing," "Taco Bell: Experience Amazing," "Goop: Experience Amazing." Empty and useless. Nike's "Just Do It" lives on and Apple's "Think Different" is still constantly referenced decades later in every meeting for a reason. They're memorable because they're perfectly, uniquely suited to their brand. Hey Lexus, bring back "relentless."

I love advertising because we believe that if an idea has been done before, and done well, you can't do it again. Hollywood believes the opposite. To them, if an idea has been done before, then of course you repackage it and do it again. Advertising has higher standards. To us, "it's been done before" is the surest reason to *not* do it.*

I love the way advertising very quickly adopts social causes, much faster than the rest of the business world.** It moves quickly to self-correct and self-reflect. Ad people really want to do good, so much so that they lunge at a good cause. Yes, this includes #MeToo, in response to which the industry immediately enacted change, because it was the right thing to do. Because advertising

---

* Is this still true? They've brought back the Geico Cavemen, the E-Trade Babies, All-State's Mayhem, and The Most Interesting Man In The World, to name a few. If you're reusing another agency's creativity, you're not creative, you're a cover band.

** Advertising embraced #MeToo in 2018 and made swift changes. In comparison, the FDIC went through a sexual harassment scandal in 2024, prompting chairman Martin Gruenberg to step down. In 2024. Whoever was still saying or doing anything sexual to anyone in 2024 is a fucking moron.

people know that if you have to be in the business world, it's best to try and change the business world.

I love people in advertising. Funny, smart, self-effacing, hard-working, creative, empathetic, hilarious to drink with. People who are delighted by ideas, fiercely protective of pop culture, and willing to debate seemingly silly details. Love.

I love my friends. To my advertising friends: as Neil Brennan said, "You're not really friends with somebody unless you're both worried that if your text messages went public, you'd both lose your jobs." You're all hilarious.

No, Intentions Do Matter

During #MeToo, and the subsequent social . . . upheaval? Panic? Correction? We heard this phrase a few times: Intention doesn't matter. Only impact does.

It's a great example of the kind of saying or mantra that suddenly takes hold, everyone repeats as gospel, and then kind of memory-holes once the panic subsides a bit. I think I understand the, ahem, intention behind this saying. But it's so deeply flawed. For a couple of solid reasons.

First, though, I understand that saying, "I'm just kidding" or "I didn't mean it" after an offensive comment is bullshit. The first job of "intention doesn't matter" is to negate these asshole comments, and I'm in support of that. If you've said something that genuinely hurts someone, you should apologize without qualifying your words with a weak "I didn't mean it." That response means you didn't think about your words, and you still don't want to think about them. Not thinking warrants an apology.

But beyond that, it gets a lot more complicated. Whenever I consider this phrase, I zero in on this horrifying gem of a comparison: What's the difference between someone who is texting while driving and runs a person over, and a serial killer? The answer is all the difference in the world. One of them is a moron who didn't set out to kill. They other is a monster who absolutely set out to kill in the most selfish, brutal, and calculated way. The impact is the same, a dead person. But the serial killer's full intention is to find a victim and murder them. That's their goal. The driver's intention may have been to let someone know they'd be making lasagna for dinner. That's their goal. Both end up in tragedy, but morally speaking, lasagna and capital murder aren't quite the same.

So, it's a matter of circumstances or context. How bad were your intentions, versus how much did you not think this through? Almost always in my own practice and with others, I focus on the second scenario and try my best to ignore the first one as much as possible.

It's like the impulse some people have to try to find conspiracies everywhere, when usually the best explanation is just dumb errors. Before attributing bad intent, I try to first ask myself, "Did this person just fuck up?"

I love philosophy as far as I can understand it,* and in particular I love The Principle of Charity. Basically, it asks us to interpret the unclear stuff in the nicest way possible. When a person says or does something that stops you for a beat, consider that argument or action with the best possible intention and meaning that you can. Building this psychological muscle helps you to identify with the kindest part of a situation and increases your likelihood of getting somewhere great—or at least keeps you from constantly ascribing horrible intentions to others and therefore being angry all day. It's a great principle to live by, and in applying it I'm slowly untangling a lifetime of uncharitable interpretations. Like, I'm not so mad at my dad anymore.

---

* Steve Martin: "If you're studying geology, which is all facts, as soon as you get out of school you forget it all, but philosophy you remember just enough to screw you up for the rest of your life."

But there are a few other reasons I really dislike "Intentions don't matter." The first is the intention behind the statement itself. Saying that one's intention doesn't matter at all removes any defense a person might have, making them perpetually, unassailably guilty. Which, sadly, seems to be the goal of many people, and most of X's (formerly Twitter). It's the cheapest, quickest way to gain power over someone, by denying any good in them. It's the argumentative equivalence of plugging your fingers in your ears, with the goal of maintaining your victory in the situation.

Let's apply it to a #MeToo moment of mine, which is what this whole thing is about.

In the very earliest days of #MeToo, I was standing on the stairs of my agency. There was a group of us talking, and I made a joke and people laughed. I put my hand on the shoulder of the woman standing next to me.

"Oops, MeToo!" I said. More laughter. Everyone dispersed. Great team. Yay us.

Except no, definitely not yay us. That woman went to HR and complained about me. And went to the CEO and complained. And in her complaint, from what I heard third- or fourth-hand, she accused me of being disrespectful and hurtful.

My intention was to make a group of people I worked with laugh. The impact was a woman feeling offended. In response, her intention was to get me in trouble, or maybe even fired. My intention thudded. Her intention succeeded.

If given a chance to see her face while listening to her point of view, I would absolutely have apologized and changed my behavior immediately going forward. Who wouldn't? But she didn't think charitably, and she definitely didn't think of coming to talk to me. My guess is she thought I would react badly, or she didn't want to see the pain in my face when I was accused of a horrible act. Or most likely, she was afraid of the consequences of challenging power. But most of all, by talking about me to someone else, she left no room for my intentions. And I think anyone on that staircase might have thought what I said was careless or flippant, but not cruel.

The principle of charity can clear up a lot of bad jokes.*

Second, when we remove someone's intention, the only thing that's left is the power of impact. There's nothing else. And, by extension, it is totally up to the person affected to decide what the scale of impact is. They have the power to quantify their hurt on any scale. Intention could modify that power, put it into perspective. Remove intention, and impact is power unchecked. Which might be the point of that saying's origin. It feeds a person's narcissism to say "My feelings are more important than anything else." Like the whole "my truth" thing Oprah pushed. Sure, it's your truth, but it's also just your viewpoint. To say "your truth" is to create a reality where your feelings trump everything else. And it denies those of anyone else involved. It denies anyone else is truly involved at all.

Third and finally, intentions do matter. What someone is thinking when they do something hugely matters. Because intentions are, and I mean this, *the most powerful things in the universe.*

Set an intention, and you put the universe in motion. Set an intention and things, people, and circumstances get behind everything you do.

If you leave your house each day with the intention of defending yourself because the world wants to fight you, you'll probably get into a fight. If you leave the house with the intention of being

* Here's something I can't get my head around. At the same time this person made that complaint, she also left a note on my desk saying what a great boss I was and how much she had learned from me. Does this mean she was unaware of how destructive her complaint was? Or was she covering all angles, afraid of my potential power to retaliate? Or did she truly believe in the rightness of both actions? WTF. I'm still spinning out over this one.

kind to everyone around you, you'll probably get a few smiles and thank yous. Intentions totally shape experiences.

Set a larger intention and you might change your life. Ask anyone who's succeeded in, well, anything. Set your focus on a clear outcome and watch the universe align things around you. There's a reason every motivational coach values intentions above everything else. Intentions are the lens through which you shape your world. It's fucking weird but it works. Ever hear the phrase "act as if"? Perform the role you want and soon you will inhabit that role. That's setting a huge intention. What is a vision board but intention-setting? What is a resume but a script that you use to get a job? Intentions make everything happen.

To say they don't matter is totally bizarre, unhelpful, unkind and inhumane. It's totalitarian to deny intentions and say that only impact matters, in that only one way of seeing a situation is the acceptable way.

I know several people who've gotten into accidents while texting. I'd work with, live next to, and smoke a joint with any of them, any day.

A serial killer? Not so much.

What is hell, but the total absence of hope?
The substance, the tactile proof of despair?
—Ken, the demon, from *Buffy the Vampire Slayer* (S3 E1)

Diet Madison Avenue

Never accept the definition of who you are
from a person hiding the truth of who they are.
—Maria Lemmo, Culinary Artist

Diet Madison Avenue was a group of people (it's unclear how many, but at one point they claimed a mix of seventeen advertising professionals and lawyers) who, beginning in late 2017 and for most of 2018, were extremely active online in purporting to expose sexual harassers in the advertising industry. I say "purporting" because it soon became obvious that achieving fame was a huge driving force for them. They seemed to revel in the attention they got, adopting a snarky tone to their posts, and using their platform to preach intersectionality and other social justice causes. They were sought out as ad critics, and at one point appeared to be *the* moral voice that the industry must heed. Their accusations were wild and totally unproven; they lived in a protected world behind anonymity, where rumor was fact and nothing could be fact-checked.* They spoke often about stepping

* From "How #MeToo Accountability Spectacles Enable Frauds: The Saga of The Punk Rock Therapist, Anti-Flag, Kristina Sarhadi, Rolling Stone, and the Enough. Podcast. Part 1" by an online blogger with the pseudonym Jack Torrance. The article is about a #MeToo accuser who turned her experience

out of the shadows and revealing themselves, but they never did. In short, they scared the shit out of people and made others cackle with glee. Then they were sued and went quiet.

I was going to write a whole chapter about DMA, but I don't want to get mired in anger or a desire for vengeance; it's not serving me or anybody who might be reading this. Despite Elizabeth Hardwick's witty quote about why we write, this book won't be about revenge. That can't be the intention here.

But I will say that I never woke up with the intention of wrecking a person's life. Never. Diet Madison Avenue did. Every day. For months. That was their intention, destroy some men, maybe even take down some agencies, and become famous. It was their intention to be mean-spirited and cruel while twisting a social justice cause into righteousness-fueled destruction.*

No wonder they want to remain anonymous.

---

into a charity/business: "The refrain to skepticism towards these kinds of public spectacles from the most ardent supporters of #MeToo is 'What would an accuser have to gain by lying, nobody would do it just for attention?' Outside of the naivety and the fact that in the age of social media attention may arguably be the most valuable commodity, the acquisition of a massive platform to launch a "charity," allegedly thousands of dollars in donations that will go directly into your pocket, a steady stable of clients and being publicly legitimized and allowed to practice as a mental health professional there is no record of you being certified as is surely an incentive." This is pretty much word-for-word about DMA.

* I met one of my accusers in a supermarket. Her name had appeared on at least two lists of members of DMA. We had worked together years earlier and I thought (my weakness again) that we had been friends. She gave me a bright, happy "Hello!" Which absolutely stunned me. I said, "I know you were one of them." She denied it. But then I quickly caught her in some lies. Then she told me she'd been sued for being in the group. I said, "Your group ruined my life." She said, "Well, lots of women have been hurt in advertising." Again, that scoreboard, notching up wins. I switched my thinking and became collaborative. Because her business was all about connecting people for productive talks, I asked her whether she would like to get coffee some time, to talk, find common ground, find a way to help each other. She laughed in my face and walked away. Let the healing begin!

Scapegoats

Scapegoating. It's one of the oldest forms of punishment. Adam and Eve were booted out of the Garden of Eden, doomed to wander. Cain was forced to wonder. Let's get a quick definition from the Bible:

> *But the goat, on which the lot fell to be the scapegoat, shall be presented alive before the Lord, to make an atonement with him, and to let him go for a scapegoat into the wilderness.*
>
> —Leviticus 16:8-10, KJV

Driving out that goat cleansed Israel for a year.

According to the interweb, before the Bible, the ancient Greeks practiced scapegoating, too. It was common in India and China. Shakespeare wrote about it; he was kind of obsessed with it. The British Empire employed it regularly during its reign as a means to gain tight control over disputed territories. However and wherever the practice started doesn't matter. What is important is that it happened all the time. It is very *human* to scapegoat.

The goats would be loaded with idols, talismans, and possessions that reminded people of the bad stuff they'd done that needed purging. They'd pile that stuff onto the goat, kick it in the ass, and drive it away. The town was now cleansed of its sins and closer to the purity of the spiritual realm. We're good! No more guilt! Beers on me!

That was the goal of the scapegoaters. Drive out their sins and stay happy. They could keep even the most perfectionist moral code intact by piling their transgressions onto a goat and driving it out. The goat's sacrifice cleanses everyone else. Who wouldn't love such a system? Everyone gets to be a little shitty knowing that an unwitting little goat will soon take the fall? Sign me up.

Except the practice of scapegoating is a lot darker than that. It's called scapegoating partly to hide the fact that they didn't always use a goat. They used human beings. People were piled with stuff, stripped, paraded around, spat on, beaten, sometimes stoned, and loaded up with the town sins, symbolically and physically. And then driven out.

Back then, scapegoating was probably cause for a celebration. Today it certainly seems to bring people together. There's a sense of joining a cause, a feeling of community. "Hey everyone, let's get this one!" Nellie Bowles said in her book, *Morning After the Revolution*:

> To do a cancellation is a very warm, social thing. It has the energy of a potluck. Everyone brings what they can, and everyone is impressed by the creativity of their friends. It's a positive thing, what you're doing, and it doesn't feel like battle, but like tending the warm fire of community. You have real power when you're doing it, and with enough people, you can oust someone very powerful.[12]

What a rush it is! It's the modern-day equivalent of Neanderthals coordinating to take down a woolly mammoth.

We must remember that banishment from one's village often meant being banished from one's entire world. Everyone you knew, the only place you'd ever lived, the only source of food you knew, everything, gone. It almost always meant death, from starvation, exposure, or wandering into a hostile area. But sometimes people died of loneliness. Here's Salman Rushdie, summing it up terrifyingly as Moraes Zogoiby gets booted out of heaven in *The Moor's Last Sigh*:

> The gates of Paradise were opened, and Lambajan averted his eyes. I stumbled through them, giddy, disoriented, lost. I was nobody, nothing. Nothing I had ever known was of use, nor could I any longer say that I knew it. I had been emptied, invalidated; I was, to use a hoary but suddenly fitting epithet, ruined. I had fallen from grace, and the horror of it shattered the universe, like a mirror. I felt as though I, too, had shattered; as if I were falling to earth, not as myself, but as a thousand and one fragmented images of myself, trapped in shards of glass.[13]

Or here's Shakespeare, from *Romeo and Juliet*, Act 3, Scene 3:

> There is no world without Verona walls,
> But purgatory, torture, hell itself.
> Hence "banished" is banish'd from the world,
> And world's exile is death; then "banished"
> Is death misterm'd. Calling death "banished,"
> Thou cut'st my head off with a golden axe,
> And smilest upon the stroke that murders me.

Banishment sucks. But who cares? Fuck Romeo and Moraes, right? Cindy Gallup, one of the self-appointed moral consciences of advertising, has said more than a few times that she didn't care about the careers of a few men when compared to what women have gone through for decades. And yes, that seems fair, but it's also a pretty obvious admission that those few men are taking the fall for an entire industry's malfeasance. That's scapegoating.

Scapegoating works because it gets everyone else off the hook. The whole can breathe a sigh of relief after a few have burned. Could have been me, wasn't me, now I can go back to a quiet life. The storm has passed and I survived.

The *Quillette* editorial board wrote a piece about the May 2022 firing of a Princeton professor named Joshua Katz. He'd had an affair with a student, been reprimanded, and served his time. Then Katz began vocalizing opposition to some university policies. And because he did so, they reopened his harassment case and fired him. And no one supported his right to oppose their policies or questioned the fact that he had already been punished. Why? Because it's *so much* better to stay quiet. As stated in "The Disgraceful Firing of Joshua T. Katz" in *Quillette*: "One of the most powerful corrupting forces in human affairs is the desire for a quiet life. It leads good people to join mobs they don't support and to be spectators to injustice."[14]

Those are the same mobs that cheer and dance when the goat is driven out. Gotta love that quiet happy life. Make gobs of money in white-collar industries like Hollywood, journalism, academia and yes, advertising. Jobs that aren't physically back breaking and offer plenty of opportunities to drink and hook up. Jobs that allow them to fly around the world, dine out constantly, meet celebrities, get tickets to everything, and create movies and ads and papers that make people smile and make them feel that they are doing good. No way does anyone want to shake that up. They have mortgages to pay.

And the last thing they want to see is the goat walking back into town reminding them of who they really are.

The Morning Show

Ted: So, I just finished watching the first season of Apple TV's series *The Morning Show*, and I have some thoughts.
MeToo: Right there with you, big guy.
Ted: I thought you'd want to do this with me.
MeToo: Just keeping you honest.
Ted: It's a good show, at least when it stays on the topic of #MeToo. The acting is great, and it wrestles with the issues in nuanced and complex ways. And the scene where Steve Carell barges into the show to plead his case to the people he worked with *devastated* me. That's how I felt about Droga5. I loved everyone there (well, almost everyone) and could also feel the anger, reluctance, and complicated feelings of everyone looking back at him.
MeToo: Agreed. I was worried it would be too sympathetic to Steve Carell's character, but then that scene. . .
Ted: Yes, the scene where he takes advantage of the young producer.
MeToo: Say her name.
Ted: That's funny. A young producer named Hannah Shoenfeld, in his hotel room. For someone reading who

hasn't seen it, Steve Carell plays a Matt Lauer-type named Mitch Kessler . . .

MeToo: Type? He is basically Matt Lauer.

Ted: OK . . . who befriends a young producer while they are on assignment together at the Las Vegas shooting in 2017, when Stephen Paddock opened fire on the Harvest Music Festival, killing sixty people and wounding over four hundred others. Deadliest mass shooting by a single gunman. Hannah is understandably shaken by circumstances, and she meets Mitch while out walking. Mitch offers perspective, advice, and comfort in the face of a tragedy, and the inexperienced Hannah welcomes the friendship and mentorship. Then he takes her to his hotel room and pounces on her.

MeToo: Yes. That's what needs to stop. For good.

Ted: I agree. It was awful. A betrayal of every signal and action up to that point. But wasn't it pretty obvious and un-nuanced? The show is praised for its sensitivity, but that scene was so predictable, or rather, the melodrama was very scripted-for-TV, not real life.

MeToo: Yeah, but that is what happens in real life.

Ted: Well, sometimes, but damn. It was so obvious that she wasn't responsive to his advances and didn't feel good about any of it. And aren't other situations grayer than that? He basically raped her.

MeToo: Yes, he did. Here was a man who'd had anyone he wanted and who was so sure of his power and attractiveness he could do anything and get away with it.

Ted: But it was *so* obvious she hated it. If he was any sort of normal person he would have stopped what he was doing.

MeToo: No. You don't get it. The show *had* to portray her feelings on the outside, they had to show her experiencing that pain for the camera, because in real life women are conditioned *not* to show it. We laugh at your dumb jokes and don't push away your advances out of fear and exhaustion, but inside we feel like Hannah. Inside we freeze and take it. And we have had enough. So, if she was being too "obvious" for you, that's because you were watching a TV show where you can't read people's minds. They have to act it out, dumbass.

Ted: Fine, call me a dumbass. And I was dumb. I had much milder situations like that, not ever in hotel rooms or forced sexual conditions, but situations in bars and at agency parties where I thought the laughter was genuine, I thought the flirting was real. Was it?

MeToo: Maybe sometimes it was. But maybe other times it wasn't, and the woman across from you was playing a part so she wouldn't fall out of favor with you. Maybe sometimes she did laugh and did kiss back, and yet still felt like Hannah inside. Do you get that?

Ted: I do.

MeToo: That's why workplace flirtations and relationships must stop. It's impossible to untangle the complicated power dynamics from any romantic situation.

Ted: But sometimes laughing and making out is just that, sometimes it was fun. I'm not blind and I'm pretty empathetic. I truly believed that every time I was with a woman it was fun and consensual. I wouldn't have done anything otherwise!

MeToo: Power clouds it. It just does.

Ted: I thought the subplot with the weatherman and the young British producer was a great illustration of that. She thought she was in love with him, but really, she was in love with the forbidden nature of their affair. Once it became public, it lost all its thrill.

MeToo: Yeah, that wasn't real love, it wasn't good, it wasn't healthy. This workplace nonsense needs to stop; it's damaging.

Ted: I hear you, but . . .
MeToo: Oh god.
Ted: No, I have another point.
MeToo: What is it?
Ted: What about all the workplace relationships that lead to real romance, marriage, and children? Some of the best relationships I have ever seen started at work. Nearly everyone in advertising met their spouse at work or in the industry.
MeToo: "In the industry" is different from a direct working relationship.
Ted: Yes, it is, but the dynamics are still there, just fainter. But many, *many* advertising marriages started in the same office. And 99% of second marriages did, too. Some great marriages began between people working in the same place.
MeToo: So, you're defending workplace relationships?
Ted: I'm saying that it's going to happen whether people want it to or not. And maybe we need a better way of dealing with it instead of demonizing it. In 2019, the CEO of McDonald's was fired for a workplace relationship that was reported as consensual and replaced with that CEO who can't seem to stomach the Big Arch burger.[15] The Nestle CEO was fired in 2025 for an affair, and the shrapnel from that is still flying around.[16]
MeToo: You can say I'm in denial, but business and love shouldn't mix. In fact, the Gen Z move away from wanting to spend ridiculous amounts of time in the office supports this thinking. Work should be a small part of life, not consume it.
Ted: But in a world concerned with safety, are Tinder or Hinge really better than meeting someone at work?
MeToo: Yes, they are. Work should be safe. We need a big shift.
Ted: And I would argue that policing peoples' feelings is inhuman and inhumane. We can't control how people fall

in love. We can't. Maybe we need a better system to allow relationships to happen, because they will happen. To paraphrase Thanos: "It is inevitable."

MeToo: What?

Ted: Sorry, Marvel reference.

MeToo: Figures you're a Marvel nerd. But you talk about virtues like forgiveness and empathy. What about the virtue of controlling your impulses for the good of those around you? Remember when you get in a workplace relationship, it affects *everyone* you work with.

Ted: Yeah. It does. I had an old boss who refused to hire anyone who was in a relationship with someone already working there. He thought it was so destructive.

MeToo: Boundaries.

Ted: Boundaries.

MeToo: You are the poster child for why we should set boundaries. Yes, someone might find love, but also someone could torch a promising career. Let me ask, if you could go back and do it again, would you honor much stronger boundaries?

Ted: Jesus, what do you think?

MeToo: Boundaries. Here you go, quote boy, here's one from a musician named Phil Good: "When someone oversteps your boundaries, they're letting you know that what you want doesn't matter."

Ted: That makes sense.

MeToo: You got mad about boundaries before, how about: "If someone throws a fit when you set a boundary, it's just more evidence that the boundary is needed." I don't know who said that one.

Ted: I get it, and I didn't get . . .

MeToo: David W. Earle: "Boundaries represent awareness, knowing what the limits are and then respecting those limits."

Ted: I . . .
MeToo: Pamela Cummins: "Individuals set boundaries to feel safe, respected, and heard."
Ted: OK, I get it.
MeToo: Do you?
Ted: . . .
MeToo: Boundaries.

AgencySpy

I think it began with AgencySpy.

AgencySpy was/is a website for the ad industry. It publishes articles, creative reviews, promotions, and general insider news about the industry. It was owned at one point by *Adweek*, which perhaps felt that a gossipy news site would allow their contributors to be a bit snarkier than they could be in the magazine.

But most of all, in the years between 2004 and 2016 or so, AgencySpy gained popularity in the business because of their comment sections. These comments were the first place people in the industry went to, in order to be mean as fuck about each other. And most important, they could be *anonymously* mean as fuck about each other.

Being mean used to come with the territory in the ad world. Talking trash about a competitor or their work was normal. Expressing disdain or cynicism was totally expected for a creative. "Dude, that ad sucks. That copywriter is the fucking worst." That was a very normal, somewhat healthy way to express a jaundiced professional opinion about a colleague or competitor in passing — in office hallways, at parties, by surreptitious texts, or whatever. Those comments usually hid jealousy, creative insecurities, or personal grudges. They were a way to express complicated feelings, such as, "Is that person actually a better creative than me?" Or, "Am I secretly a total hack?" Or, "If that person wins an award does it mean the universe hates me?" Or, "Will my existence collapse if someone I dislike gets a better job than mine?"

AgencySpy brought that professional bile into full view of everyone. And pretty quickly it was a big hit. With AgencySpy, as with the Internet in general since 2005, your own personal hatred suddenly flourished in full view of thousands. For those from my generation, older or a little younger, this was new. And really shocking. Anytime someone was called out, people reacted. Angry narratives were built within minutes. People would claim not to have read anything, then say something that revealed they had definitely read something. Friends I had were devastated by hateful comments. Two guys I knew were each convinced that the other was writing negative comments about him. Both swore they weren't; both swore they knew the other one was. This was pure poison. I know this all seems like the normal Internet of today, but back then it was incendiary.*

With AgencySpy, the industry entered a crueler, angrier age. Like the boiling frog, we all didn't feel it at first, but as the heat turned up, the cruelty became normal, which meant the average person carried around dark, jealous, hateful thoughts and was more likely to express them or fear them from others. Again, coinciding neatly with the growing tide of *all* anonymous Internet comment sections. Fun!

AgencySpy posted "news" that was designed to get angry reactions, and more than likely joined conversations under anonymous pseudonyms to stoke the fires in comment sections. AgencySpy

* I can still remember the first hateful comment about me: "What has Ted Royer ever done besides eat?" Which is succinct and funny and a totally fair question. And to my face, it would have made me laugh. Reading it from someone anonymous just made me sad.

thrived on the hatred in the comments. AgencySpy's hate made it stronger. More generously, AgencySpy probably saw itself as a journalist-crusader-activist site, bravely taking on the evils of the world by exposing the faults of nerdy, insecure advertising creatives. Net-net, AgencySpy was more responsible for amplifying the industry's internal hatred and cruelty than anything else.

I hated AgencySpy. I felt it was just one more thing pulling apart our industry. And I *really* believed that ours was an industry that needed to hang together, to pull for each other. The fact that, as mentioned earlier, two very good creatives who both did excellent work were growing more and more suspicious of each other indicated to me that we needed to be reminded of our common goals. Forces were ripping apart advertising from every direction.

Whenever I was asked to give a speech, I talked about Our Tribe. It boiled down to the following points:

1. Really there are only about one hundred agencies in the world that can claim they truly care about creative work. The rest say they do, but do they live it?
2. This means there are probably only about 5,000 people around the world who *truly* believe in the power of creative advertising ideas above all. You know who you are, and you know if you're someone just going through the motions.
3. Clients are losing respect for us. Long-term agency relationships are becoming shorter and shorter on average. Project-based work (work that has singular limited scope and time period) is on the rise. Both of these trends have gotten worse. Even now, the role of Chief Marketing Officer is getting phased out and marketing is becoming far more fractional, where your day can be divided into multiple jobs and income sources.
4. Research shows that no one from Ivy League schools is going into advertising anymore.

5. New technologies are being invented every day to ignore what we do. Ad skipping is becoming quite the thing.
6. Because of this, the small tribe of ad people who were doing great work and who cared about great work should be sticking together versus tearing one another apart.
7. Agencies themselves shouldn't undermine respected competitors. Creatives should be happy when someone else does a great piece of work, because it makes our industry better as a whole. At times, I even quote Freud's theory of "the narcissism of small differences." Like-minded agencies that have tons in common should find more ways to help each other thrive, because no one else is going to help them.

That was pretty much it. It always went over great and, more importantly, I *meant* it. Our industry was getting pummeled from all sides; it didn't need to punch itself in the face.

With that spirit in mind, I went to an Ogilvy party for something or other around that time and was in a pretty good mood until a PR woman I worked with approached me.

"Hey!" she said in a cheerful way that meant a request was to follow. "Billy Tindersnitch wants to meet you." Tindersnitch was an editor for AgencySpy.

I answered, "I do not want to talk to that piece of shit," or something equally tactful and measured. Clearly, I do not have the ninja/judo skills required to make it to the top; a true C-suite type would have met him with a smile and done everything to win him over. An enlightened person would have considered that Tindersnitch was doing a job, chasing the clicks he needed to chase. A generous person would have found a way to sympathize with his situation. I mean, he was at a swanky Ogilvy party on an *Adweek* salary. That would make anyone resentful. I, however, did not possess the ability or empathy to see beyond my own sense of righteousness. After having given my speech a few times at events like this one, I was filled with the protective fire of loving and defending our industry. This was a big mistake.

"That motherfucker is more responsible for increasing the industry's internal hatred than any other human being alive," I said, patiently and rationally.

As (truly) tactful as ever, the PR woman smiled, said she understood, and went off to relay that news to Tindersnitch. I watched as she walked over to him. He watched me as I watched. I watched as she told him I didn't want to meet him. He watched me watch him react to not wanting to be met. I watched as his body tensed with anger. He watched me pretend not to be watching but obviously still watching. He watched me being very happy with myself and my choice.

And it just made everything so much worse.

Comments about me on AgencySpy ramped up in viciousness. I was an AgencySpy villain within weeks. It got so mean I had to stop reading.

Eventually, and for some reason unknown to me, AgencySpy had to delete all anonymous comments. You could feel the industry breathe a sigh of relief. (Most people I knew responded like me: "Good, now we can just go back to making ads again.") But simultaneously, people looked for another outlet for the anger that had become so normalized and proved to be powerfully addictive. One commenter wrote, "AgencySpy was the only forum we have to speak truth to power!" As if agencies were run by suppressive dictators and not insecure nerds. That commenter proved to be far more prophetic and modern than I wanted to admit, for it's very common today to see work as oppression. I would have called this stance absurd, and I would have been deemed a dinosaur for it.

Lo and behold, Fishbowl came along and quickly thrived in a way AgencySpy never had. Fishbowl is a site anyone can go on anonymously and talk about almost any industry. The advertising section is robust. With the advent of Fishbowl, users could start their own threads on any subject they wanted, and say anything about anybody—again, anonymously. Powerful people, and agencies, could apply pressure and get comments deleted, but most people had to take it. Meanness had firmly taken root, settling in for good.

Later, and much worse for me, it turned out Tindersnitch was either a member of Diet Madison Avenue or a huge supporter of it. During the #MeToo furor and attacks, AgencySpy posted regular updates about DMA, and got DMA's opinion on everything ad-related, from new hires to the social justice supporting content (or lack of) in ads just released. He clearly was orchestrating or at least hugely supporting their plan to become the new Voice of Advertising Moral Authority.

I'm positive he never forgot our nonexchange at the Ogilvy party. What I thought was a dunk on an asshole attacking our industry was probably the birth of a nemesis, plotting and planning my demise. Stupid me. All politicians know: hold your friends close and your enemies closer. Duh.

In one article about #MeToo after my firing, Tindersnitch wrote, "And not one of these men has ever apologized for anything they have done." Whenever I've had a chance to speak to a group, in a speech, and certainly in conversations I've had with individuals since, I've apologized to anyone, anywhere, that I may have offended, and offered my email, tedroyer50@gmail.com, to discuss whatever I could to make it right. No one took me up on it. I even went to a conference in Las Vegas, stood on a stage before a roomful of angry people, and apologized.

Tindersnitch never reported the apologies.

A Conversation With the Universe

Ted: Hello, Universe?
The Universe:* Yes, Ted, hello.
Ted: Hi. I don't talk to you much. Not really since I was in my 20s.
Universe: I know. But we are here now.
Ted: I didn't believe in you. I didn't believe in a higher power.
Universe: I know.
Ted: And then I was one of those "new atheists" like Christopher Hitchens and Sam Harris, who rejected the idea of a sentient force out there who cared for us or gave a toss about what we did.
Universe: Yes, I remember you thinking that.

* Meet the other voice in my head. The Universe is meant to provide wisdom and perspective. This isn't nearly as problematic as #MeToo, but that's not for me to decide. I talk to both for a good amount of time each day. "Let us examine the question together, my friend, and if you can contradict anything I say, do so and I will be persuaded," said Socrates. Well, no one else wants to talk to me all day about this, so my imaginary friends will have to do.

Ted: Also, I was extraordinarily mad at you for turning my cousin Mark into a quadriplegic. As you know, he broke his neck while swimming in the ocean. That was shitty.
Universe: Yes, Ted. I understand how angry you were.
Ted: Well, like you say, I'm here now. I've been doing a lot of therapy, thinking about a higher power, and I think I need to start talking to you again.
Universe: You can always talk to me.
Ted: I'm struggling to understand what happened to me.
Universe: Go on.
Ted: Like, what the fuck? I thought I was a good boss and a good person, on the whole. And I feel like a train hit me.
Universe: I understand that you are feeling that feeling and having those thoughts.
Ted: Can I rant to you? I can't really rant to anyone.
Universe: You can rant to me. I'm listening.
Ted: I can't rant to anybody. I can't rant to my friends because I'll just become boring and bitter. And even though I feel boring and bitter on the inside, I don't want to seem boring and bitter to everyone else.
Universe: I totally get it.
Ted (takes deep breath): OK, here goes, because I'm going to unload this on you.
Universe: Ready.
Ted: IT'S TOTALLY UNFAIR. All of it, every bit of what happened to me. I don't know how to defend myself. I don't know how to move past this. I don't know how to recover my sense of self or gain any sense of how to move forward.
Universe: I understand. And I think . . .
Ted: So many other people have done so many worse things than me and they are fine, their careers are fine.
Universe: I hear you.

Ted: It's bullshit! And everyone knows it, but no one is willing to say it in any sort of public way. Oh, in private literally everyone says, "You took the fall for all of us," but in public they all have to pretend to agree that I deserve to die.
Universe: Well, not *die.* I understand it feels that way to you, but have you—
Ted: Why me? WHY. ME. I know a guy who slept with his staff and paid them millions of dollars for their silence. He's fine. I know another guy who repeatedly offered money to a production rep to sleep with her. His career is great. I know a woman who hit on several staff members, and she's sailing by, her career is just dandy. But I'm wrecked.
Universe (pauses): Well. . .
Ted: Does anyone give a fuck about me? Does anyone want to hear my side? Everyone is just having fun feeling pure and thanking *you* that it wasn't them who went down.
Universe: I can help you if you are willing to calm yourself and listen.
Ted: OK. Yes. Fine. Of course I'll listen.
Universe: Have you realized that these thoughts you're thinking, they are just thoughts?
Ted: What?
Universe: The thoughts of doom and hopelessness and what everyone else thinks about you, these are just . . . thoughts. They aren't real.
Ted: What are you talking about?
Universe (sighs): Here it is. Taking control of your thoughts is taking control of your life. Our worldview is only understood, defined, and acted on through the lens we choose to see it through. These lenses act as a filter for the entire world. If you choose to see pain and fear, you will experience pain and fear. If you filter in love, you will experience love. If you—

Ted: Dude, are you serious? My career is *destroyed.* I can't get a job *anywhere.* That's *real.* And you're talking to me about thoughts and lenses?

Universe: It's the main . . .

Ted: You know where I am right now. I'm in bed. I can't get up. I can't move. There's an ocean of darkness spreading out where my future should be. There are real people actively seeking to really keep me unemployed and ruined. Real people. And you're talking about thoughts.

Universe: I understand. This is the way to move—

Ted: Forget it. I'll talk to you later. I'm going to take some antidepressants now.

Universe: OK. We will talk again. I am here when you're ready.

Ted: Yeah. Sure. Thanks for nothing.

With Power There Is No Consent

"With power there is no consent." This is the phrase I kept seeing at the beginning of #MeToo. It's the phrase that made me sit up and really take notice.

With power. Yes, sexual harassment has always been about the exercise of power. We watched it in every training video. You know, the one where the guy running the trucking company cuts the woman's routes because she won't sleep with him. Or the one where the guy says something really offensive and the woman complains, and then *she* gets shipped off to a new, worse job in Alaska. I, like you, watched all of these and couldn't believe how stupid men were to do these horrible things.

Let me start by saying that I never saw myself ever as a man with power. Yes, I had a big job title and stature in the industry. But I never acted alone, always had checks everywhere, and worked under what was basically a senior committee of decision-makers. I had no authority to fire anyone or move them off an account without approval.* I had to justify decisions. I am inclined to listen and

* I know there are people out there who worked at Droga5 who flatter themselves that, if it hadn't been for me, they would never have been fired. Sorry, you would have. The whole organization had to agree and approve. It was

incorporate different points of view, and I often criticized myself as being weak because I did that so often.

As a creative, I identify as someone who dislikes power, rails against it to get the best ideas sold. I believe in the rebellious spirit of creatives, and you can't be a rebel and be in charge at the same time. Creatives are always fighting the forces in society that don't want adventurous, dangerous, dark, funny work. Among my industry friends we would often laugh at what we'd gotten away with, the work we sold that had an edge to it, the amount we got paid for being outrageous and crazy. We thought we were pulling the wool over everyone's eyes, and anyone who believed their own bullshit was a poser. We were business outsiders, court jesters, artists among the bean counters. My first boss, Tom Monahan, used to say, "We are the rock 'n' roll of the business world. A meeting with us has to be the most fun part of a client's week." Maybe this was delusional and self-serving,* but it's how I, and many around me, felt.

But I will admit that I never seriously reflected on the fact that, as I earned more authority, money, and fame, I became more "attractive" to women. I put attractive in quotes because it wasn't just me who was attractive,** it was my status and title and experience that added to it, for sure. I knew it but didn't think about it. Sooo, any flirting that happened, I would tell myself, "Wow, she genuinely likes me." Or, "Wow, I'm getting more handsome with age." Or "Wow, MDMA makes me really fun." And I did not, decidedly did not, chalk it up to the power I had. Yes, this was stupid and delusional.

---

always a group decision, approved at the highest level by everyone after long, carefully considered reviews. Sorry.

* It was.

** Hey, before you get mean, I can be pretty fucking charming, despite the enormous square head.

There is no consent. OK, but *none*? How can that be? How can we know the level of anyone else's consent? Consent exists in someone's mind. Can we really say consent disappears entirely in the face of power imbalance? As I wrote before, does the "no consent" nullify all the marriages and families and babies conceived from an imbalanced power dynamic? It emphatically does not.

I'm old. I'm from the past. It's a big knock against me in a very ageist industry. I grew up in the '80s. And every '80s movie had, let's call it, a problematic view of consent. *Sixteen Candles* and *Revenge of the Nerds* both contain scenes that are basically rape, with "consent" coming only after the victims react ridiculously by falling in love with their rapists. This was considered comedy in the '80s. This was considered comedy for *teenagers*. Stolen kisses? Totally a thing back then. It was *romantic* to steal a kiss. And to everyone who was there at the time acting now like that wasn't true back then, you're lying. John Cusack was hailed as a romantic icon for not leaving his ex-girlfriend alone but instead standing outside her house blasting music. Unwanted kissing is now considered assault. Blasting music outside someone's house is now considered stalking.*

Times change, and that's a good thing. Everyone needs to learn to accept that as they pass into older years. What was young and cool becomes outdated and weird, sometimes even contemptible.

If you asked me at any time in my life, though, I would say I had full consent from others in what seemed truly like mutual attraction, and I would also say it's monstrous, *monstrous,* to imply that I would settle for anything other than that. I never felt any rush of power when I flirted. Never. I believed in romantic escapism, not power. Advertising was a very promiscuous industry, and it attracted the kind of person who believed life can be boring, work

* Even if it's Peter Gabriel's "In Your Eyes," one of the most romantic songs ever written, it's still stalking, Lloyd.

can be dull, and we're only on this planet for a short time, so we might as well spend it making great stories and getting drunk with colleagues. That's not evil. Advertising people *loved* to hook up. Until they didn't and pretended they never liked it in the first place.

But today the definition of consent has shifted to support the statement "with power there is no consent." Since being fired and doing all the work I can come up with (again, let me know if you have other ideas) I have come to change my opinion about dating at work: *Don't do it. Ever.* But . . . there will still be happy relationships with power imbalances baked into them. There will be families and babies and retirement together for couples who met at work and who overcame the policy that implies they were committing a monstrous social crime by falling in love. Eventually, "With power there is no consent" will become one of those phrases like "Never trust anyone over thirty," and "Wives submit to your husbands as to the Lord."* That will be more an indication of the time they came from than a lasting moral truth.

I think a lot these days about morality and truth. I realize that I am, by the nature of my age and my actions, outdated. I have felt wrong. Very wrong. Horrible. Disgusted with myself. And very, very guilty of things I've seemingly committed with the power I had, which by definition means there could be no consent.

But I heard something several years after the fact, which was a startlingly good take on morality, youth, age, and shifting standards. It's from a poet named Darby Hudson on TikTok, and he puts it better than I can.** Here's my favorite bit by him, a scathing take aimed squarely at me, advertising, and all the young people so quick to condemn others:

* The Bible. It's loaded with doozies like this one.

** He's at @darbyhudson6, and further proof that TikTok is an astounding evil genius creation, in that normal everyday people can find incredible philosophers in between golden retrievers and car crashes. I can't stop.

> Between the age of twenty and thirty-five is a time when the culture disorients you, recorrects you, makes you lose sight of your childhood by teaching you to blame it and steals the magic from your mind's eye. So, it's no surprise that advertisers spend most of their money aimed at the twenty-five- to thirty-five-year-old crowd. They con you into believing you're the main character by selling you a quick fix. Life stories and instant anthems to buy into, and praise from your true self. And twenty to thirty-five feels like you're never going to age and time is on pause, so of course you'll believe you're the main character. You're practically immortal. And people over 40, they seem like they're born old. It's understandable to think you're at the end of history, because YOU have arrived. So, it's natural to believe that anything you change will better the world forever. Become an activist, go to a protest.
>
> But time has tricked you. Science evolves. Big ideas change, and morality was always fast fashion. And soon you're shat out the other end and quickly become part of the great tradition of fucking it all up for the next generation. Born a hero and die a villain.

As your villain of the moment, as someone who was immortal in my twenties and thirties, and as an advertising professional, I can attest to all of this. Morality is often just fast fashion, just you watch. Watch as the world changes around you and you get caught flat-footed. Watch as you slowly realize you aren't the star of your own movie; you're just another person trying to figure it all out, and unexpected shit hits you in the face.

I had power. I thought I had consent. I thought I understood it. That reality changed right under me. I guess that makes me a bad person.

I Am a Bad Person

Roseanne Barr was a Bad Person, but she is slowly becoming a Good Person again. Slowly. Will Smith was a Bad Person, sort of, but then he forgave himself and then he went onstage as the Fresh Prince so he's becoming a Good Person again. Donald Trump is a Bad Person who can't seem to get cancelled—every attempt to cancel him makes him stronger, which is astonishing and disturbing and unique in the world. Kevin Spacey is a Bad Person. He was found not guilty in court and I think no way is he coming back, but we'll see. Mark Wahlberg (allegedly) beat a man almost to death, blinding him in one eye, but he did it when he was young, and he is a Good Person for sure. James Franco is currently a Bad Person. Bill Clinton is a Good Person who will probably only become Bad after he dies. Lizzo was accused of sexual harassment by her dancers, but has it made her Bad? She showed up two weeks later at an event right beside Beyonce and got kudos on X. That's some fast forgiveness right there. She seems permanently Good to me. Lori Loughlin cheated the college admissions process and brought shame upon herself, her husband, and her daughter. Yet she's being cast again. All Good! Matthew Perry was almost universally considered Good. During this writing he was accused of beating his ex-girlfriend.

He started to be Bad, but then he died and now he's Good. Andy Cohen, too, has recently been accused of stuff, but he has powerful Good armor. I suspect he'll skate through and retain his Good status: we will see him again on New Year's Eve.

If you are a Republican, then according to the Democrats you are racist and misogynist and a Bad Person. You're always Bad or about to be Bad. If you are a Democrat, according to Republicans you suffer from woke mind viruses and other delusions and are irredeemable until you take the "red pill." So you are Bad. Democrats can become Bad pretty quickly. Andrew Cuomo was being called presidential material when he got #MeToo-ed hard. Weirdly, that was what took him down even as he faced (in some opinions) a much worse scandal in hiding the number of deaths in nursing homes during COVID. But #MeToo was the story, and #MeToo took him down. My guess is his #MeToo stories got many more clicks. #MeToo is a click-getter as well as an efficient Good-to-Bad conversion tool.

In advertising, there are very few Bad People. Joe Alexander was the CCO of the great Martin Agency. He was #MeToo-ed, loudly and publicly, and some women denounced him.[17] According to the people I know in advertising, he is a Bad Person with no chance of redemption ever. Martin Sorrell* was sort of a Bad Person for about a month and then started a new company so he's not Bad anymore. Ralph Watson, an insanely talented art director, got #MeToo-ed at the same moment as me, and he also seems to be permanently considered a Bad Person.[18] I don't know.

* Martin Sorrell was for years the most powerful man in advertising. As Chairman of WPP he regularly made headlines with his enormous bonuses. Also, he always walked onstage in Cannes to collect the Network of the Year trophy, something I thought should have been a bit beneath him—like, dude you have a host of people who'd be so thrilled to have the exposure, let them go up. But whatever. In an early #MeToo moment, Sorrell was fired, allegedly for using funds to pay for something nefarious. He called the allegations bullshit. No one remembers it anymore.

I am a Bad Person. I am wearing the pig nose. But I used to be a Good Person. I did campaigns for gun control and The Gender Pay Gap. I put gay people in ads when it was still somewhat controversial to do so. I did a campaign for *The New York Times* centered around the word "Truth." According to my left-leaning community I was Good. Then I got #MeToo-ed and overnight I became Bad. It doesn't help that I *look* like a Bad Person. I am white. I am over fifty. I have a gut, the result of years of a sedentary lifestyle and a deep, lifelong love of Ben & Jerry's. I dress poorly, in that I wear the standard old-ad-guy outfit of all black: black t-shirts, black athleisure pants, black shoes. My head is block-shaped, like a newscaster from the '60s. I look like the patriarchy. Therefore, the chance that I could become Bad was greatly increased. And when I became Bad, people took one look at my face and were like, "Yeah, that figures."

At any moment in the public eye, people are considered Good or Bad. This is binary and bizarre, because people are way too complicated to be judged in this way. But we do judge. We've always done this, I guess, but with the Internet and the socials, the Good-Bad judgements are all-pervasive and never ending. In *The Coddling of the American Mind*, Jonathan Haidt points out in a part titled "The Untruth of Us Versus Them" that:

> Life is (seen as) a battle between good people and bad people . . . (there is) a larger cultural narrative that creates an 'enemy' who must be fought against using all available means . . . It is up to you and the rest of the good people of the world to fight them. Assemble a coalition of the righteous and shame the evil ones until they change their ways.[19]

Chuck Klosterman wrote a book about being Bad, *I Wear the Black Hat*. It's about villains in society and why they are labeled such. The book has a chapter on Hitler, a person who by near-unanimous consensus is the ultimate Bad Person. Klosterman's take is smart and funny because he admits in a self-aware way that he can't even write about Hitler. Hitler is *so* Bad that writing about him is walking into a tightly packed minefield. Much of the chapter is an acknowledgment that the chapter itself probably shouldn't exist. That's some deep Bad. But even now we see some crazies out there trying to nudge Hitler toward Good. Hitler.

Lindy West is a very funny writer and author of one of my favorite articles of all time: "I Rewatched *Love Actually* and Am Here to Ruin It for All of You." It's amazing. West would probably dislike me for being on the wrong end of #MeToo, but the movie *Love Actually*, we can very much agree, is awful. Wretched. The worst. It's creepy and immoral and reduces humans to simplistic caricatures at best, dangerous psychos at worst. And in her article, West nails the idea of people being either Good or Bad:

> *Love Actually* puts a lot of stock in the idea that people are either good or bad. People either love or they don't, reciprocate or they don't. The grander the gesture, the greater the crime of not reciprocating. LOVE GOOD. NOT LOVE BAD. It's a nice fantasy, because if, instead, you accept the difficult truth that people are more than just good or bad, then you have to question whether or not happiness really exists. Because if people are more complicated, then happiness must be more complicated, and at that point, is it really happiness?[20]

The Good-Bad binary is a problem both ways. Labeling someone Bad reduces them to unsalvageable trash. But labeling someone Good brings its own challenges—mostly blindness. Leaders considered Good are less likely to be held to the same standards of behavior, making it easy for them to transgress without being called out for it or caught in the act. Sam Bankman-Fried fooled people because he seemed so Good. He spoke a lot about doing good in the world and expressed how much he cared about the right things to the right people, which greatly added to the blind trust people put in him. From futurism.com about his trial:

> In particular, he (Fried) was a vocal proponent of "effective altruism"—the vague but noble concept of using data to make philanthropic giving as targeted and helpful as possible. But in direct messages, when Vox's Kelsey Piper observed that Bankman-Fried had been "really good at talking about ethics" . . . he responded he had "had to be" because he's been engaged in "this dumb game we woke Westerners play where we say the right shibboleths and everyone likes us."[21]

Bankman-Fried was convicted of fraud in 2023, accused of taking around $10 billion from investors. Pretending to be Good at the cool cost of 10 billion.*

Author and NYU professor Scott Galloway, when interviewed about the tendency to describe people as a "net positive for society" put it this way: ". . . the problem is with the word 'net,' and that is, once we decide an individual or a company is a net good for society, we don't want to hold him or the company accountable for anything."[22]

We let Good people off the hook all the time, until they tip over into Bad. Right now, there's someone you might consider to be Good who someone else thinks is Bad, or Very Bad. And neither

* Incidentally FTX did a Super Bowl ad that was well made, but then became unintentionally hysterical. It featured Larry David as a character who throughout history is skeptical of obviously great inventions like the wheel and portable music. When we come to the present day and someone shows him FTX, he says, "Nahhh, I don't think so." It's rare for an ad to so totally collapse into itself and emerge with a completely new meaning like that one did.

of you wants to budge, because budging shakes the narrative. So, is Lizzo Good or Bad? Russell Brand? Elon Musk?

Plus, and this has been magnified by the immediacy of the phone in our face, it's *weird* to hate someone you don't know. Anyone could find it easy to think of someone they despise just because they've been declared Bad, even though they have no personal experience with that person. I used to hate Meghan Markle. I have zero personal experience with her and every bit of my opinion comes from media, news and her cloying show. She might be awesome in reality. I don't know. Now I try not to hate her. To waste energy in hating someone because of some narrative that's worked its way into our thinking can't be normal, healthy behavior for the human mind. Especially in a world that wants us to hate, for the clicks.

Good and Bad, with a few exceptions, is in the eye of the beholder.

When I look at people now, I try to get past the temptation to think in terms of Good-Bad. And I've met a lot of both. I've shaken hands with pop stars and presidents and sat across the table from murderers. I was nervous around all of them. And paid close attention to all of them. I often saw a common thing in all of them, whether they were radiating confidence or pleading for understanding. What I see isn't Good or Bad, just humans trying to make sense of all of it.

If we divide everyone into either all Good or all Bad, there is no acceptable outcome other than total victory. Frodo and Sauron didn't sit down and see each other as fellow beings with valid points of view. Harry and Voldemort didn't find common ground. Destruction was the *only* outcome for these narratives. It's either you or me. Kill or be killed. That makes for great stories, great narratives. And a terrible way to live.

I'll end with a thought from a man who spent most of his life ground down by the Soviet boot. It's a line that for some reason seems to piss some people off, which astounds me. But I guess they don't want their Good-Bad narrative taken away from them.

The line dividing good and evil runs not through states,
nor between classes, nor between political parties either—
but right through every human heart.
—Aleksandr Solzhenitsyn

The Righteous Rush

The surest way to work up a crusade in favor of some good cause is to promise people they will have a chance of maltreating someone. To be able to destroy with good conscience, to be able to behave badly and call your bad behavior "righteous indignation"—this is the height of psychological luxury, the most delicious of moral treats.

—ALDOUS HUXLEY, FROM *CHROME YELLOW*

We are in a "culture of outrage" because the magnitude of rage is, in fact, overtly outrageous. And it is righteous.

—ALYSSA MILANO, IN A TWEET ABOUT THE #METOO MOVEMENT

Holy goodness gracious criminy zoinks, did that Huxley quote rip me up when I first read it. Although Huxley published his novel in 1921, is there a more apt summation for our time? Just go on X or whatever and you'll find moral righteousness flung all over your eyeballs. Every comment dripping with indignation and righteous fury. Each typed out with sweaty fingers completely sure of their own correctness and everyone else's wrongness.

It feels *amazing* to be righteous. You feel huge. A force seizes you and pushes you out beyond yourself. You're infused with crackling energy. Your path is clear, your conscience is clean, and you have the power to lay waste and feel *triumphant.*

Religions are fueled by righteousness. Soldiers need it to kill. The SS troops in World War II had belt buckles that said "Gott Mit Uns"—God Is With Us. The most organized mass murderers in history were like, "Yeah, we're the good guys" because of righteousness. Yikes.

And people banging away on keyboards get potent hits of righteousness as they fling their comments into the ether.

The righteous rush is reinforced in our culture all the time. Liam Neeson movies and video game narratives, reality shows and country songs about cheatin' spouses. Characters infused with righteousness are exciting, because of one quality: they have full license to do serious damage. In any other context, Neeson's violence in *Taken* would be psychotic, sadistic, and deranged. But because they have effectively framed the villains as unredeemable monsters who deserve the righteous fury brought down upon their heads, Neeson's wrath is thrilling, fun, and cathartic. Kill those Albanians! But wait, first break their arms, shoot them in their legs, and then kill them!

News and social media *love* to frame certain people as monsters and therefore release in us the thrill of the righteous rush. You hated Claudine Gay?* Maybe you feel that rush, and you get to inundate her and her family with racist hate messages in the name of taking down the enemy. You despise Trump? Then you get to hurl any abuse at him or his supporters you want to.

The problem with the righteous rush is simple: people are *not* simple. They are complex. They are living, breathing, walking

* The ex-president of Harvard who insufficiently condemned antisemitism and allegedly plagiarized a portion of her academic work. She became a polarizing figure very quickly, another person caught up in the endless culture wars.

gray areas. They can change their minds. Then change them again. They can make horrible mistakes without meaning to.

The rush obliterates any grayness. There's no rush if one has to stop and think and maybe even be generous in one's calculations. Have you ever thought that maybe one of the guys Liam Neeson murdered was just a cousin who was just hanging around the baddies for that day? Or maybe a guy who desperately needed money to feed his family, so he winds up working with awful, seedy characters, but he didn't know how bad their behavior was? Nope, no way, that saps all the fun from a Neeson killing spree.

But grayness is what makes humans so interesting! It's why shows with complex characters grab and surprise us. In *Game of Thrones* (at least in early seasons), a character could transform from awful villain to sympathetic hero in a matter of episodes. In *Mad Men* everyone was a mess, but oh so recognizable as human and flawed. And *Succession* was brilliant at creating characters who were both hero and villain at once, switching even in mid-sentence. Those writers whipped your righteous rush up and then clipped it when you least expected it. It was disorienting and wildly entertaining. And human.

Social media is the ultimate test kitchen for the righteous rush. People look for outrage to participate in because it feels awesome to bathe in anger. Condemn the Bad and feel Good. Reacting or responding to anything with outrage is the new Great American Pastime. In this example, the commenter feels a tiny little rush as he or she responds:

> Question on Quora: *Why Do So Many Murderers Bury Victims' Bodies In Their Own Back Yards?*
>
> First comment posted: *Not everyone has the trunk space or gas money to drive way out in the middle of nowhere to dump their bodies. Check your privilege. We're all doing the best we can out here.*

OK, it's obviously a joke, but dead on.

I had a friend in an agency who faced that righteous rush. He was speaking to his creative department and he invoked the dreaded Louis CK. My friend described the way comedians always save their best joke to tell last, and how CK would take that best, last joke and make it the first one, so he had to better it with everything that followed. Good story, very relevant to advertising creatives, or any creative person for that matter. Don't rest when you have your best idea; make it the benchmark that all subsequent ideas have to beat. Guess what happened next?*

Think what you will about Louis CK, and I have a variety of feelings about him as well, but it's undeniable that he's an excellent comedian and writer. Maybe the best standup ever. But he is a Bad Person. And my friend journeyed straight into Bad Person territory for just mentioning him. HR meetings, tears, and simmering tensions ensued. People used the invocation of Bad Louis CK as an excuse to ride the rush. My friend had handed them a gift. Invoke a Bad Person in any context other than how Bad they are at your own peril, because you've just activated the rush. My friend never really recovered from that moment; he was fired some time after.

The test kitchen of narcissism will constantly provide a gold rush for the ego. We see it every day, as people glom on to causes, using them to feel that amazing rush for themselves and their superiority to others. Nothing hits like the righteous strain of that superiority drug. To feel righteous is to be bathed in the confidence of one's power. And what good is power unless you can use it on someone? As my friend Justine Armour, CCO and a great creative says, "It's *always* been about power. Always."

Huxley's quote nails it. Feel the righteous rush, and you can use your newfound power to hurt *anyone* and get away with it.

---

* Isn't it amazing that you guessed correctly?

Isn't that the history of religion in a nutshell? Believing that God is on your side (Gott Mit Uns!) gives you permission to do horrible things. Substitute "righteousness" for "religion" and Nobel-winning physicist Steven Weinberg's quote from 1999 immediately becomes modern: "Good people will do good things, bad people will do bad things. But to get a good person to do a bad thing you need religion."

The righteous person is a superhero, in his or her mind. Unstoppable, ready to bash the bad guys. But more often than not, that superhero is more Homelander from *The Boys,* and less Captain America from *The Avengers*. Pure ego looking to soothe itself, instead of sacrificing for the greater good.

In 2016, Chuck Klosterman published an incredibly interesting book called *But What If We're Wrong? Thinking About the Present As If It Were the Past.* What if what we believe today is wrong, misguided, or even evil? What if future generations look at what we were doing and *hate* us for it? How often does anyone stop and think like this? I think about that book's premise every day. In it Klosterman writes:

> I think there's a greater detriment with our escalating progression toward the opposite extremity—the increasingly common ideology that assures people they're right about what they believe. And note that I used the word "detriment." I did not use the word "danger," because I don't think the notion of people living under the misguided premise that they're right is often dangerous. Most day-to-day issues are minor, the passage of time will dictate who was right and who was wrong, and the future will sort out the past. It is, however, socially detrimental. It hijacks conversation and aborts ideas. It engenders a delusion of simplicity that benefits people with inflexible minds. It makes the experience of living in a society slightly worse than it should be.[23]

I love that quote. Even if I disagree with the "slightly" part.

When Morgan Spurlock's documentary *Super Size Me* came out, the ad community loved it. For thirty days, Spurlock, a fit, healthy teetotaler ate nothing but McDonald's food. He deteriorated quickly. In one powerful scene, his doctor (who, weirdly, also happened to be my doctor) told him that after a week of a strict McDonald's diet, Spurlock had the liver of a hardcore alcoholic. *Super Size Me* was an inspired, purpose-driven take on fast food. As ad people we loved the way Spurlock creatively took down one of the most obviously unhealthy and egregiously mass-market clients who (at the time) was doing bland work anyway and was (at the time) not on board with commissioning great creative work. I stopped eating McDonald's. (Mostly. I mean, c'mon, those fries.) Many people I knew stopped eating it completely. We were all disgusted; how dare McDonald's poison us all like that? Overnight, McDonald's became the target of a fun-but-serious righteous rush.

But what if we were wrong? Turns out, it seems that during the filming Spurlock really was an alcoholic.[24] If that's true, he'd done the damage to himself well before putting McDonald's on trial. In 2006 a group of students recreated *Super Size Me*'s experiment after Spurlock's alcoholism was revealed, and except for mild weight gain, they were pretty much unchanged. Think of the millions, maybe even billions that film's lie cost McDonald's.

Of course, to get the biggest, longest-lasting rush, you need to create something everlasting, something that is impossible to prove even exists but *feels* like it does. For example, the Soviets created the amorphous, ever-pliable charge of "foreign agitation." This was an unfalsifiable crime that could be applied to anyone, anywhere. On the surface, it meant that a person was acting on behalf of foreign powers to bring down the Soviet Union, but everyone understood it was nothing but a blunt excuse to apply state power however and whenever the government wanted. It was an all-encompassing, totalitarian "Because I said so." The charge of foreign agitation was elusive, and it was eternal. It could never be fully proven (those clever evil foreign agitators!) and it could never be snuffed out (we must be ever watchful!). This elusive, eternal enemy was very, very handy in justifying *anything.*

If you want to work up a crusade, it's best to have an ever-present eternal enemy hiding around every corner. And new ones are being created every day. The Patriarchy fits well. Communism is a solid, blobby, old chestnut. Zionism always makes its comeback. Unconscious bias is a *great* one. Unconscious bias is kind of the perfect Elusive Eternal. It lives in everyone's brain and is so slippery no one actually knows when it's there! Deny it's there, though, and that only proves it's there. If it floats, it's a witch.

A collective of people afraid of an elusive enemy and feeling the rush can do horrible, horrible things. Look no further than any moment in history ever. But George Carlin said it succinctly: "I love individuals. (But) I hate groups of people who have a common purpose . . . 'cause pretty soon they have little hats, y'know?"

And hashtags. And armbands. And flags. And slogans. And lists.

I know, and I see every day, that society can make us numb, disconnected, and scared. As I write this we're well into 2025 and I've never been more aware of crazy reactive thinking. There's a ton of hate and fear, and violence too. C-suite people are being shot and the Internet cheers. The rush fuels everything bad, gives it strength, pours gasoline all over any bad situation. I would love for all of us to practice what Klosterman advocates in his book: humility and wonder. And I'd love to jam an enormous syringe into America and draw out the righteousness, and then inject a huge cocktail of gentle humor, communication, and forgiveness. But I'm old and fired and probably shouldn't be making any drug analogies.

Beware the Narrative

The Universe: Maybe it's not about righteousness. Maybe it's about belonging, not feeling alone in your pain.
Ted: I guess. Especially the pain part. Doesn't anger come from pain?
Universe: Yes, it does. And what soothes pain more than feeling you are cared for? Feeling you are not alone?
Ted: So, for that brief moment someone is slinging hate on the Internet, they really are trying not to be alone?
Universe: Possibly.
Ted: A lot of the discourse does get down to an us-versus-them feel.
Universe: So, if you really try not to see good versus bad, but flawed humans, maybe the righteous rush, as you call it, is really about people feeling connection, even in condemnation?
Ted: OK. Is that where my anger comes from? Feeling alone?
Universe: What do you think?
Ted: It certainly makes sense. I get angriest when I see the world moving on without me. I'm feeling left behind. I think it's at the core of who I am now.

Universe: Not who you are, but how you see things. It's a narrative you've told yourself and one that you've really bought into.
Ted: Yeah, the narratives we build are very powerful. I hate them.
Universe: Hate is a strong word.
Ted: OK, mistrust, I deeply mistrust them.
Universe: Go on.
Ted: Narratives.
Universe: And why do you mistrust narratives?
Ted: I would hear this line all the time from a former colleague: "What's the narrative here?" She was a very senior person who loved to get everybody on the same page with "the narrative." Didn't matter if the narrative was a lie or straight-up manipulation; what was most important was getting our story straight for what she considered to be the unwashed masses, who were not worthy of hearing the truth. "What's the narrative here?" was a rallying cry to gather around a story, a version of events we could all agree to. It was permission to bend the truth and manipulate in the service of a greater good. In most cases the greater good was usually a placated client and subdued, productive workforce.
Universe: I understand. Maybe she just wanted peace and consensus. As you like to say, "People love to pay their mortgages."
Ted: Yeah, but I felt gross hearing that word, "narrative." I deeply distrust misleading narratives when I sniff them out. That'll happen to a person when they've lived with a massively distorted narrative built around them.
Universe: Understandable. People find comfort in narratives. It simplifies a scary world.
Ted: But it's almost always so manipulative. Politicians want to "control the narrative." News stories are biased depending

on who is telling them. Our culture is full of spun-out, shady narratives. Writing on truthdig.com in 2024 about the 2012 UVA Phi Kappa Psi rape case, which turned out to be completely false, journalist Freddie deBoer said:

> It's really genuinely difficult for me to imagine a culture less conducive to free inquiry, controversial opinions, and uncomfortable truths than that which has governed media in the past decade or two. You had an elite media that was dominantly made up of left-of-center and Democratic voices, with a steering committee of that elite class that was even further left-leaning . . . . And you had Twitter, which made all of this public, had direct quantitative indicators of which opinions were popular and which weren't, created a permanent record, and allowed for periodic communal charivaris that demonstrated the crowd's ability to inflict punishment.[25]

Douglas Murray, a British writer and journalist, and a conservative, says the world is more dangerous now than ever because "we don't have a difference of opinions, we have a difference of facts." We have a difference of narratives. And advertising *worships* stories and storytelling.

Universe: Story is a good word.
Ted: Chuck Klosterman said this about stories:

This is the difference between the fox and the hedgehog. Both creatures know that storytelling is everything, and that the only way modern people can understand history or politics is through the machinations of a story. But only the hedgehog knows that storytelling is secretly the problem, which is why the fox is constantly wrong.[26]

Universe: I like saying "story," because most of these narratives are stories we tell ourselves, don't you think? Remember, we talked about thoughts before, that they are just stories, our ego making sense of things.

Ted: Ugh. I have so many: I'm a monster. I can't succeed. People are totally selfish. I have to win awards. I'm ugly.

Universe: Yes. Sometimes our narratives are good for us, and sometimes horrible. Your guy, Aldous Huxley, said that narratives when "treated as absolute truths, are dogmas to be swallowed and idols to be worshipped, and can lead us into all kinds of inappropriate behavior."

Ted: My previous narrative of how awesome I was led me into some inappropriate behavior.

Universe: You know what he means. These are what a writer named Gay Hendricks in *The Big Leap* calls "Limiting Beliefs." People construct a story around themselves until that narrative becomes their actual reality, like the scaffolding around a building that obstructs the real view.

Ted: They feel real.

Universe: They're supposed to. And we can say narratives are collective thoughts. They can collectively motivate or harm. Sometimes both.

Ted: They're scary.

Universe: If you allow them to be. Or you can take a step back and recognize them for what they are. Did you see the *Barbie* movie?

Ted: Yeah. I went to *Barbie* ready to hate it. I had a feeling that it was going to feed into some man-hating narrative, but the kids wanted to go so I went. I freaking loved it. It was hilarious, inventive, and subversive.

Universe: It's really good! And there's a line that kind of flew under everyone's radar that's relevant for discussing narratives.

Ted: "There are no multiples of Alan. He's just Alan."
Universe: Ha, no. It's when the creator of Barbie, Ruth Handler, says, "We make up things like patriarchy and Barbie to deal with how uncomfortable it is to be human."
Ted: Oh yeah, great line. We do make them up. And they suck. They hurt us. "There is only one God" is a narrative that's resulted in a shit ton of murder. "Believe All Women" was terrifying to me. So, any woman can say anything about me? Cool. Awful.
Universe: Narratives can affect others by being unempathetic. Holding on too tightly to a narrative is an inherently unempathetic act. Sinking into your own narrative closes off the possibility that absorbing another narrative can truly help one to grow. It allows a person to live in a comfortable fantasy, and, again, hurt others and not feel bad about it. Famed author Susan Sontag has something interesting to say about stories from an interview she did in the '80s.
Ted: Uh-oh. Wasn't she a feminist?
Universe: Yes, but to your point, her story is very complex.
Susan Sontag: Hello.
Ted: Hi.
Susan Sontag: I'm always struck by the fact that there is a kind of ambiguity in the very notion of storytelling. On the one hand, we think of storytelling as a truthful activity. "Tell me the real story." We think of stories as bringing information, as revealing secrets. But we also think of stories as "that's only a story" or "don't tell me stories," meaning don't tell me lies. And don't you think at the very center of the whole enterprise of storytelling there is the fact that it is an activity that faces simultaneously in two directions? On the one hand, it's connected with an idea of truth; on the other it's connected with the ideas of invention, imagination, and lies. One is thrilled by a story precisely because it describes

something that seemingly can't happen. It's connected to fantasy. I think it's all so, so complicated.[27]

Ted: Dude. I completely agree.

Susan Sontag: Thank you.

Universe: You just called Susan Sontag "dude."

Ted: I'm sorry, I apologize. It's just something I say for emphasis. But yes, I really agree. It's so complicated. #MeToo wasn't just complicated. #MeToo was also righteous.

Universe: But some narratives heal or help to dissipate the pain. To many, the #MeToo narrative was a story that told us we could become better, that men and women can coexist better, we can heal. Maybe that story had to begin with such a crushing shock against complacency to jolt the world awake. To some that violent impact meant hope.

Ted: I know. I feel that. I certainly didn't want to be on the wrong end of something so positive. I want to hope. I want to change. The world showed me I need to be open to change. I feel exhausted. I feel like surrendering.

Universe: That's not a surrender, that's growth.

Ted: These narratives are little worms that burrow into our heads, fed to us from news and social media and movies and our parents when we're four years old, and they stay in there, growing along with us and convincing us they *are* our personalities. Then we unfollow people who disagree with us or disown family members because they don't fit into our established narratives. How the fuck do we fight that?

Universe: There is one way.

Ted: Meditation? Mushrooms? Ayahuasca?

Universe: You wish. Wisdom.

Ted: Oh god, that sounds like a lot of work and time.

Universe: Yes. Socrates said, "The only true wisdom is in knowing you know nothing." It takes a massive dose of perspective, experience and hard-earned humility to realize you don't know much at all. How can one person? The world is massive, ever-changing, and too complex for your recently evolved monkey-brains (yes, I, the universe, acknowledge evolution). You, Ted, created all sorts of narratives and they blew up in your face—that part doesn't happen to everyone. Now you get to create new ones. And when you see through the narratives often enough, you start seeing their structures. You understand that there's *so much more* to know.

Ted: So that's why young people get so fired up when they learn a narrative. When my niece was five, she learned from an adult that you should *always* turn the lights off when you leave a room. She then proceeded to yell at everyone who left a light on. Young people with total belief in one strong idea scare me.

Universe: Wisdom comes with age and experience, and with it one develops the ability to see past a single narrative and draw on experiences that challenge its ferocity. Young people are often frustrated with older generations' lack of passion and anger, not realizing that when you've seen and experienced a ton of life, you're much less inclined to jump onto a narrative.

Ted: But wait, aren't intentions just narratives we are trying to create?

Universe: I guess I would say an intention is meant to propel you in a direction, where a narrative can reinforce or block movement. Our job is figuring out which is which.

Ted: OK, so wisdom is the goal. In which case, to achieve that goal is to know nothing.

Universe: More or less, though to put it another way, the goal is to become humbled by the knowledge of what one does not know.

Ted: Actually humbled, not LinkedIn humbled.

Universe: LinkedIn humility is not real-life humility.

Ted: I just had a thought. Imposter Syndrome is the feeling that you don't really know anything compared to others, and that you'll be found out, right? Like, "I shouldn't be in this job, I'm a fraud."
Universe: Yes.
Ted: And usually, Imposter Syndrome is the result of a lack of confidence.
Universe: OK.
Ted: But if ultimate wisdom is the realization that I don't really know anything, then couldn't Imposter Syndrome just be wisdom manifesting itself? Like, it's early onset wisdom? Maybe it's not a lack of confidence, but the creeping knowledge that we *don't* know everything, and as we grow older, we realize we know less and less?
Universe: That's good! The ego can't comprehend the not knowing (or the illusion of not being able to know), so it invents the concept of being an imposter.
Ted: Deep. Getting back to work, with employees, coworkers and especially creatives, I hated having to give them any sort of narrative. There's a scene in *The Right Stuff*, the movie adapted from Tom Wolfe's novel about the Mercury astronauts and America's first few missions into space, where John Glenn's capsule is orbiting Earth and experiencing some difficulties. The scientists at Mission Control don't want to panic him, so they recommend controlling the "narrative" and keeping the truth from Glenn. Alan Shepard, another astronaut, hears this and becomes livid, saying coldly, "He's a pilot, you tell him the condition of his craft."
Universe: You love movie quotes, don't you?
Ted: I'm Gen X, we speak in movie. In other words, instead of spinning narratives to make situations go away in the workplace, maybe it's better to be honest with the people you're hurtling through space about the condition of the

craft. If your company or team is facing a serious problem, does it help to hide it, or is it better to respect your people enough to share the gravity of the situation?

Universe: I've often found that giving people the trust and respect to know what the conditions really are motivates them to go above and beyond to help solve the problem. It's good to trust.

Ted: That's risky, though; we live in a world where entitled tattletales run to online spaces like Fishbowl and spill any secret they can.

Universe: Sounds like a place where people are collectively trying to make sense of things.

Ted: Yeah, it's a narrative factory all right. A mean one.

Universe: If you let the narratives get to you. Or recognize them for what they are. Freeing yourself from narratives is hard. But with practice you learn to let go and it feels pretty good.

Ted: I'm trying, man, I'm trying.

Universe: And that's all you can do. Stay with it. Try.

Where There's Smoke

MeToo: So, you're saying that we built a narrative around you?
Ted: Yes, that's part of what I'm saying.
MeToo: Diet Madison Avenue said there were twenty-five complaints against you. That's not a narrative. That's proof.
Ted: What complaints? Where? What proof? That's a number they threw out to hurt me. It's not backed by any evidence I'm aware of at all. A few social posts, and they'd built a narrative. Clearly, they were ad people, they used visuals with real impact. They would screen-shoot spreadsheets. What looks more authentic and data-driven than a spreadsheet?
MeToo: It wasn't based on nothing.
Ted: I don't know that and you don't know that; no one knows that except them. That's what a good narrative does, it fills in the blanks for us, so that we think we understand the full story.
MeToo: Where there's smoke there's fire.
Ted: Yeah, I have a friend who loves to say that. But he's wrong. It's not a valid expression anymore. There are entire industries built around us just to create smoke and spread

misinformation for personal gain. There's a whole lot of "the earth is flat" smoke. The Flat Earth Society has hundreds, maybe thousands of members. And they throw out as much smoke as they can. Do you believe that the earth is flat?

MeToo: Well, you would say something like that. Take responsibility for the fact that you created a ton of your own smoke.

Ted: Yes, I did. I definitely did. But they lit the fire.

MeToo: Out of your smoke.

Ted: So, you're OK with the narrative superseding the truth.

MeToo: I'm OK with the narrative that protects women, and if a handful of men had to go down to achieve that goal, then yes.

Ted: Easy to say when you're not the one taking the fall.

MeToo: Yeah, it's also not easy when you've been sexually harassed. Sometimes constantly. By men like you.

Ted: "Like" me.

MeToo: Like you. And *you*. You're part of the system. You take the hit. You love military analogies. You're a soldier in a war. Maybe you don't kill anyone. Maybe you hate war. But still, you put yourself in the line of fire anyway. A grenade got you and not the guy next to you. Boom. That's war.

Ted: But this shouldn't be a war.

MeToo: Like Alyssa Milano said, "Our cause is righteous." Righteousness is worth going to war for.

Ted: I can't help seeing her as an example of righteousness gone off the rails. I don't want to go to war. I never did. I wanted to make ads and get drunk and flirt.

MeToo: In this war that equates to being the enemy.

Ted: I know that now. OK, I surrender. I don't want to fight anymore.

MeToo: Great, but you're a POW now. Your release hasn't been negotiated.

Ted: When will it be?
MeToo: Don't know. That narrative hasn't been written yet.
Ted: Funny.

Worry is creativity's idiot twin.
They both make up shit from nothing.
—Darby Hudson again (he's really good.)

Badasses and Dumbasses

Turn on your TV, and soon enough you'll see an ad with a married couple in it. And chances are, and I mean excellent chances, like the 1992 Dream Team chances of winning gold, that the man will be an idiot. A bumbling husband who can't figure out how some new device works. A moronic father as he stumbles through some game his kids love. A clueless coworker who is doing it all wrong. Cringe! Douglas Murray addressed it in a Father's Day article for *The Free Press*:*

> There (is a) thing you can always predict with 100 percent certainty if a family, any family, is featured in an advertisement . . . that the man . . . will be portrayed as an incompetent or a loser. If the problem is wrestling with the remote control, the children and wife will patiently have to show poor old dad how to work the darn thing. It is a small but significant example of a wider trend . . .[28]

---

* I purposefully edited out of Murray's quote his observation that the couple is always biracial. Why? Because, holy fuck, I'm in enough trouble already without wading into racial politics.

Murray is right, but I think he's a bit behind on this. Men have *always* been portrayed as morons in pop culture. In sitcoms this has consistently been true. Jackie Gleason was the prototype in *The Honeymooners.* Fred Flintstone, his cartoon doppelganger, was always fucking up. *Bewitched*, *King of Queens*, *Everybody Loves Raymond*, *Mad About You*, *According to Jim*, *Family Guy*, *George Lopez*, *My Wife and Kids*, *King of the Hill*, *Malcolm in the Middle*, *Home Improvement*, *The Simpsons*, *Family Guy*—all portrayed men getting themselves into ridiculous situations their wives often have to bail them out of. Even in shows where everyone is crazy or stupid (*Married . . . With Children*, *Modern Family*), the dads are always a little bit stupider than the rest. It is a decades-spanning trope.

In advertising, a woman is portrayed as clueless only when there is another, smarter woman alongside her to balance things out with savvy and brains. Conversely, if your ad is there to portray hope for the future, it will depict the positive, shining face of a young girl, smiling slightly as she gazes into the distance, often backed with golden-hour lighting. Want to convey confidence in an ad? Here's how: open on a young woman as she's about to walk into an interview. Pause as a moment of doubt creeps across her face. Then watch her realize, *you can do it, gurl!* as she takes a deep breath, smiles at her ability to overcome anything life throws her way, and confidently strides into the room, presumably to get that job and to show that boring patriarchy what they have been missing.

The dumb guy is a trope I played into self-deprecatingly at work all the time, and still do as a dad. In the office, I often made fun of myself—how dumb I was, how silly, how much smarter the people around me were. This was all done in the hope that my self-effacement would put people at ease and remove tension. Did it work? Or did it just make me more vulnerable to invidious criticism? Probably both. But a lot of men play the fool to disarm others. What are dad jokes but self-effacement to charm and empower kids to trust that they are safe with us? It's a societal norm: guys play stupid and then everyone else shakes their heads in exaggerated exasperation. And fun is had by all. One agency owner I knew even said it out loud all the time for effect: "Women are just better. They are." And we would all laugh and dutifully nod our heads as good cast members in this long-running performance.

Isn't anyone getting bored of this? No, let me ask specifically, aren't *women* getting bored of this? I know some men are, because the phrase "mediocre men" is being used *a lot*. How, the phrase seems to infer, could we not have seen that the workplace is full of mediocre men? All the easier to push the self-effacing idiots aside and make room for the badass women.

I have always wondered, don't women find this communication trope of "man dumb, woman smart" to be condescending? Do women need this characterization force-fed to them? Anyone who needs to be told they are amazing . . . well, isn't that an indication of weakness rather than strength?

My theory is that's why the movie *Bridesmaids* was such a huge smash. Kristen Wiig is the funniest person alive, perhaps because she is never afraid to be the butt of the joke. She's often compared to Lucille Ball, another hugely popular star of her own show who also made herself the fall person in every episode of her shows. Wiig and Ball deserve to be lauded for not needing society to kiss up to them by constantly telling them how strong and smart they are. They show how strong and smart they are by bravely playing the fool.

I'm infinitely aware that this trope isn't the only one that applies this narrative, and that women were subjected to many harmful stories fed to them alongside this relatively benign one. Lindy West had a good summation of the power of such stories on young minds, and what she is saying could apply to the above:

> Everything is a product of its time, and the whole point is to make the future better than the present. People make mistakes, and people grow, and culture grows along with them. I'm not so narcissistic to think the media of my youth was trying to poison me or that there's nothing of value in things that hurt me. This is an imperfect history, anyhow, because there were strong women all around me, too, on screen and off, but figuring out who you are is always a triangulation of what you know and what you see.[29]

West makes a great point about triangulation; we are all a product of the stew that's fed to us.

Take pop music.* Pop hits today are almost uniformly songs about how amazing the singer is, or how the singer thinks *you* should know how amazing you are. They're an avalanche of self-congratulation and narcissism. Do we really need to have "I'm amazing" piping into our heads all the time? What is this doing to our brains? In the movie *High Fidelity*, John Cusack's character has an insightful point of view about music from the '60s to the '90s: "Nobody worries about kids listening to thousands, literally thousands of songs about heartbreak, rejection, pain, misery, and loss. Did I listen to pop music because I was miserable? Or was I miserable because I listened to pop music?"

These days, the question logically becomes: Do we listen to pop music because we constantly need to feel amazing? Or do we constantly need to feel amazing because pop music says we should? If you need to tell me how great you are, you're probably not that great.

Murray's article says the men-as-dolts portrayal is an overt attempt to demoralize men and socially engineer us to be a more feminized society. Whoa. That's a hell of a conspiracy theory! But

* Jesus, I sound old.

I think (at least in advertising, because I was there) it's not nearly as insidious as that.

It's not a conspiracy, it's laziness. It's so much easier to make the man a buffoon and the woman smart because that's the easiest way to get something sold through in a meeting, and therefore approved, and therefore produced, and therefore out in the world. It's reflexive. It means people can just do their work, the meeting will go well, and everyone can go home. And if the whole process will go more smoothly because the optimistic face of the future in the presentation is a young woman and not a young man, make it so and let's get out of here. We've got dinner plans!

I'd bet on human carelessness over conspiracy any day. I always think if someone sees a conspiracy, maybe they're just seeing the result of laziness. And the old trope of men being stupid and women being amazing isn't so much a conspiracy as it is lazy. I played the fool myself because I was (maybe too) confident. Who's more confident, the person who plays the dumbass or declares they're badass? Doesn't true equality mean women can be idiots too?

But given who I am and what my cancelled status is for, I realize that it's entirely idiotic of me to even write this chapter, and therefore I am falling into the stereotype of a blundering male moron. What can I say, life imitates art.

Daemons

Scott Scobey (not his real name) was a grumpy guy who worked in the office right next to mine.

When Scott was working on a brief, he would work alone in his office, door closed. When he was ready to print out his ideas, he would hit the print button, and then *sprint* to the printer, grab his pages, clutch them tightly to his chest so no one could see them, and scurry back to his office. Scott thought his ideas were so good that if anyone even got the tiniest glimpse of them as they came out of the printer, they would instantly be stolen. Scott often accused people, including his creative partners, of stealing his ideas. Suffice it to say, at least during the time we worked together, Scott Scobey was not viewed as a good collaborator. No one wanted to work with him. And he didn't produce much. With the "my-ideas-are-gold-and-everyone-wants-them" attitude he became a creative who no one liked or wanted to help. He signaled that work wasn't about ideas; it was about himself.

Scott wasn't wrong in one sense: credit is the creative's coin. Credit for ideas is how we build ourselves and our careers. Yes, we could all see that when Scott had an idea, it was his. But the ancient Greeks would disagree with Scott.

They believed that a being called a daemon gifted the idea to him.

To the Greeks, the daemon offers an idea and it's that person's choice whether to take the idea, nurture and grow it, or discard it. Which meant the Greeks believed that ideas were swirling around in some sort of collective psychedelic subconscious ether, and daemons were collecting them like bees collecting the pollen from flowers, pollinating our brains with an idea, hoping we would look after it. How many times have you had an idea and thought, *that's great*, and then not acted on it? Hundreds? Me too. And how many times have you seen an idea in the world and thought, *I had that idea, dammit, I never acted on it*. Well, there's proof that the daemon took the idea and found the right person, eventually.

What if we don't own ideas when we have them? What if we're gifted them, and it's up to us to care for them? Isn't that a lovely way for creative people to look at ideas? Do the daemons choose their idea-receivers based on any criteria? That would make sense, and it would seem logical that if this weird bee-flower-brain system were true, a daemon would choose the person most likely to bring an idea to life.

When the artist Mark Rothko unveiled his work, "Untitled (Red)," the story goes that someone pointed out that it was just red paint on a canvas. "I could have done that," they said. Rothko replied, "Yes, but I did." Mark took the gift and ran with it. Somewhere a couple of daemons were fist-bumping.

Paul McCartney said, "Every time I come to write a song, there's this magic little thing where I go, 'Oh, oh, it's happening again.' I just sit down at the piano and go, 'Oh my God, I don't know this one,' and suddenly there's a song." The daemons seem to *love* Sir Paul.

When a creative agrees to take ownership of an idea from the daemon, it's their responsibility to nurture it to life. The daemon chose that particular person. The pact is between daemon and human. Unless you're that person's creative partner or ally in getting it made, all other humans should acknowledge earthbound credit. The extraordinary thing about this whole daemon scenario is the way it removes the ego from the process. Creatives, and those who work with creative people, know that often someone will fight for their idea, or defend their idea past the point of its original value, to protect a fragile ego. Whether an idea lives or dies becomes too personal. That's not helpful to the idea or to the problem the idea is trying to solve, or to the opportunity on which the idea is trying to capitalize. "A great many people think they are thinking when they are merely rearranging their prejudices," says David Bohm, an American-Brazilian-British scientist.

As a creative director, when concepting with a team, I always felt it was my job to give away any idea I came up with to the team on the project. It was theirs now. I loved handing it off to someone who would look after it. I think the more generous you are, the more daemon-presents you get. Cam Blackley, one of my favorite creatives, would work on projects he wasn't even assigned to and give ideas away all the time. Daemons love Cam and feed him regularly. Scott Bell, an actual Scott and one of my all-time favorite creatives, never concentrated on credit; he always concentrated on the funniest idea. Everyone was included; therefore, everyone loved to pitch in.

Remove the ego, and the creative process becomes about caring that the idea truly *works*, not *your* place in its execution. It becomes about gathering allies to help a struggling little baby idea with great potential to thrive in our world. It becomes about being an evangelist for a creative cause. The criteria with which you judge it will be clearer, the support for the idea will be more genuine, and the criticism of it from peers will fall on curious, open, listening ears. That means that criticism will be addressed free of personal ownership, and therefore more effectively, which in turn will better help that little idea to survive. It will face honest challenges that will hone it and make it better, without being propped up falsely by ego and insecurity, and inevitably, failing. There's no bigger risk than trusting your creative instincts past the limits of your ego. Also, no greater reward.

Finally, when we realize an idea is a gift and not a part of ourselves, it becomes easier to abandon it when it's clear it's not going to work. Letting go at the right time is an amazing skill. It's so hard! Maybe it's not best for you, your situation, your ego, and your looming meeting, but maybe it's best for the idea. I think we need to absorb this notion that ideas are gifts and not . . . us. Remove the ego and you can remove the combativeness that comes with it. In creative fields we see arguments all the time over which idea is best. I love taking the perspective that I'm fighting for the best idea, not just my idea.

I think we need to absorb this notion that ideas are gifts, not ourselves. And maybe we need to absorb a similar notion, that *opinions* aren't who we are either, that they are just . . . opinions.

We have daemons for our opinions—and the stories we tell ourselves about ourselves—too. It's true. Every opinion you have about the world is something you have been given or taught, by a parent, a teacher, a friend, an article, whatever. You weren't born with an opinion about race, the economy, the environment, or sexual harassment. Every single opinion in your head was delivered by something or someone from somewhere. After it's been installed there in your brain for a while, you may have even convinced yourself it was yours all along. It wasn't.

Opinions about the world don't define who you are, despite our desires to build a sense of self around them. Along the way, a person may have gained the opinion that oil is bad. That person may go on to become the kind of "activist" who smears paint on a Van Gogh in the name of stopping oil pollution. That opinion has become that person's identity. But it's just knowledge that installed itself. And it's not the end of the potential knowledge that can get in and grow.

Shirley Conran: "At eighteen I thought I knew everything, then at thirty, I realized that I knew nothing—and possibly never would, which depressed me until I noticed that no one else knew anything, either."

Socrates: "The mark of a learned person is that they are aware of how much they don't know."

Adam "Ad-Rock" Horowitz: "I'd rather be a hypocrite than the same person forever."

Vala Afshar: "As you become older, you become quieter."

Bo Burnham: "If you like talking, you might also enjoy shutting up. It's like talking except you don't fuck up everything all the time forever and ever."

Every single one of us should realize that a daemon can put a new, better opinion in our minds. That doesn't mean that you will lose something of yourself, that doesn't mean your identity is being assaulted, that doesn't mean you should be terrified of propaganda, and that doesn't mean you will somehow evaporate along with your anger about whatever it is you're angry about. It means you absorbed a new piece of information. Our minds should never be afraid of that, right?

When Scott Scobey was sprinting to the printer and, Gollum-like, clutching his precious idea to his chest for fear of losing it to someone else, he probably thought he was doing the right thing for that idea to live. But he was more concerned with that idea being *his.* He had it backward; he wasn't serving the idea, he was serving what was most precious to him. Himself.

And somewhere a very disappointed daemon was shaking his head.

Fake Family

Larry Page said Google should be like a family. And then in 2023, Google laid off 12,000 family members.

CEOs say it all the time. Company founders tell themselves it's true. Companies do things to make it *seem* like it's true. "This company is a family." "Welcome to the (company name) family."

Nope. No. Don't believe it.

A company is not a family. It can never be a family. And it's gross and weird and "toxic" and unethical to manipulate your employees into believing they should devote themselves to a company in the same way we devote our time, effort, and love to our families. Sylvia Bonilla Zizumbo, an executive coach and CEO put it this way: "Work isn't who we are. It's not our identity. Recognizing this and separating the two is really important."

But, oh man, did I believe it. From the very first days in advertising, I was told each company I worked for was a family, a close family. Every time I moved on, I was asked, "How can you leave this family?" And I got to know fellow employees as well or better than I know my own extended family, drinking with them, smoking weed with them, going on vacation with them, and laughing with them more often than any other type of family or friend. Work friends became some of my *best* friends. Confidantes and allies, closer than family. To me, advertising aimed higher than family. It was more fun than a family, more open-hearted and open-minded, infused with mission and purpose. In advertising you get to choose who to spend time with; in a family, you get what you get, and you can get very upset.

When I was fired from Droga5, oh wow, did it feel as though I had been ripped away from a family. My identity was *way* too wrapped up in my role there and the people around me. My position in that family defined my identity. So, getting fired was as traumatic as any divorce.

I was stupid. A company is in *no way* a family. A company wants to maximize your output and pay you only what it has to in order to extract work from you. A company doesn't give a shit about how you feel.

Oh, it will perform as if it does. It will rename HR to something squishy, like "People Care," or offer onsite therapy, or create trust-building resources and seminars to make you feel as though you are safe and protected. And an ad agency especially will talk about how it's all about *the people*, how much it loves its people, how important people are, etc. But make no mistake, a company does not give a fuck about you beyond what you can do for it.

In the '90s, Saatchi & Saatchi held a meeting of global executives. One of the heads of HR stood up and gave a speech about how people were the most important part of the company. Kevin Roberts, the former worldwide CEO, stood up next and said something to the effect of, "I disagree. Everyone in this company could leave tomorrow and the Saatchi & Saatchi brand would still be the most important thing. The brand." He knew the family line was BS, that the company's identity, its mission, and what it stood for were the most valuable things.*[30]

---

* Later, Roberts got cancelled. His crime was saying there was no gender bias in advertising. His point was that some people don't want to climb the

Thankfully, there seems to be growing pushback to using the word "family" to describe a work environment. And yet, even as the culture begins to swing away from using the word, companies are continuing to perform more and more of the roles that families used to, and more so than they should. The workplace is increasingly expected to implement systems that provide the emotional support I mentioned above, such as therapy services and mental health days. Performance reviews are increasingly about an employee's mental well-being, and how the company can especially accommodate and care for that well-being. Employees are encouraged to reveal more personal information and to show their "authentic selves." Being your true self and feeling emotionally supported—isn't that what a family is for?

Except dating. Companies don't want you dating because they don't want to be exposed to legal trouble. That's it. They don't care *at all* about whether or not you find love. A company would much rather block the possibility of dating to protect itself. And anyone cheering on a "safe environment" is actually helping a company to protect its *own* safety. A family would want you to find love and be happy.

A company isn't a family. Families last for life. The relationship between a company and an employee inevitably ends. A company is a ruthless organism that will shed you when you don't suit its needs. Does your family read all your emails? Your company does. Is your family planning on replacing you at any given moment, or when your work, however good it is, doesn't suit its needs? Your company is.

Here's something even scarier. Today at more than a thousand universities in the United States, an app called Maxient is

---

corporate ladder, but rather are happy where they are doing the work. It's something that seems to be true in some cases. But he *also* said he doesn't see the lack of women in leadership roles as a problem. Not the best take.

being used by students and faculty. Here is the seemingly positive, utterly Orwellian description of Maxient from its own website:

> Whether it's student discipline, academic integrity, care and concern, or Title IX matters, Maxient provides a place to easily manage records for your student body's conduct and well-being. Modern colleges and universities are complex organizations. By improving communication and collaboration across the institution, Maxient helps to identify students in need of assistance and coordinate the efforts of departments to provide follow-up.[31]

Maxient allows students to *report on other students anonymously.* As with any trend or movement that begins on a school campus, this will most surely bleed into workplaces: people hearing or seeing something they don't like (or agree with) will be able to tell on their colleagues and get them in trouble. Other apps such as SOARS and Anonymous Alerts offer similar spyware and are also proliferating. To my Gen X ears this is astonishingly shitty. Fostering a culture of secret reporting in the name of safety is scary. Totalitarian-police-state scary. Except the police are us. They got us to spy on us.

In 2016, I judged the Young Guns award show in Australia. It's a show full of student work. I was amazed that so many of the ideas entered in the show involved building surveillance structures. For example, one idea was to position motion-sensitive cameras on every street corner and subway platform in New York City and feed information to blind people. Seems nice, but the implications are kind of creepy, no? Extra cameras everywhere! It wasn't creepy to the students; they seemed to be very comfortable with being monitored. Safety above all.

MeToo: So someone like you wants to be able to operate in the shadows? What are you so afraid of?

Ted: No, I don't want to operate in the shadows. But read *1984*. According to a *Forbes* piece titled "Everything is Listening: We Already Live in a Surveillance State, We Just Don't Know It," a world of ubiquitous policing is already here:

> As consumers use more and more devices that have CPUs and are constantly connected to the internet (IoT—Internet of Things), they are exposing themselves to more and more risks that they don't even know about, nor do they have any proven means to stop it and protect themselves. And you thought Alexa spying on your dinner conversations was creepy?[32]

Where does this leave the creative leader, in advertising or elsewhere? The leader who has to construct and support an environment where other creative people can bring their best game and feel safe doing so? Up that creek filled with shit. The creative leaders I talk to say an extraordinary amount of their time now is spent mollifying employees and dealing with HR crises. Just the sort of thing parents do.

To make matters worse on campus (and soon to bleed over into the work world, I'm sure) one *Wall Street Journal* headline declared in June 2025 that "college students are using no-contact orders to block each other in real life." Cool. Block anyone who doesn't agree with you or annoys you. Freezing family members out always makes things better.

And one more thing: Advertising, like every other modern business, is just not hiring people over the age of fifty.* It's a running

---

* How do I know this? Every headhunter says so (not in writing of course, that would be stupid). And the number of over-50s who don't have a job in advertising increases every day. I went to a lunch with an old friend, aged fifty-two. He was a little late. As he walked in, he looked at me and said, "I've just been laid off." The rest of the lunch was a therapy session about how everything was going to be OK for him. As of this writing he does not have a job.

joke, but also a reality. Ageism is a huge problem. This is something even Cindy Gallup and I can agree on. Gallup in *Forbes*:

> Advertising is extremely ageist. I already know because I'd been vocal about this for a long time. To give you one particularly horrifying example that's recent, I was on the Fishbowl app [in] the advertising section, where I saw a question a senior copywriter had asked: "Have any of you been managed out of the industry because of age, and at what age?" I was horrified. The answers were thirty-two, thirty-four, thirty-five, thirty-seven, thirty-nine, forty. Staggeringly young ages.[33]

The over-50s who do have jobs buy into this anti-other-old-people stance totally, because they of course think they are singularly valuable and totally deserve to have jobs, while the older people who don't have jobs, don't. Advertising is happy to shut out the people who have dedicated *decades* of their lives to the industry (not to mention earned decades' worth of wisdom and experience). Imagine if you aged out of your family. Sorry Gram-Gram, we need your seat at the table.

A company wants you to believe they are taking their responsibility seriously to deal with employees on the emotional level that a parent cares for a child yet will also secretly plot to encourage every child to spy on one another and report back what they don't like, and then secretly plot to remove any child when convenient. Also, you'll age out soon. And we're reading your texts. Oh, and no dating.

No wonder no one wants to return to the office.

Snowflake or *Vyzhivshie*?

Speaking of unfriendly work environments.

In 2023, I freelanced as a consultant for an interesting creative company. It was very enjoyable work. I helped the company define its mission and creatively express who it was and what it believed. The female owner and I got along extremely well, and I looked forward to doing as much as I could for her, not just for money but mostly because my appreciation for her and belief in what she stood for was boundless.

And then it got worse.

An employee saw my name on a purchase order and *exploded.* This person was shocked that their company would have anything to do with me. They quickly spread the news to everyone else, and a staff revolt began brewing. How could this be? How could someone let a monster in the building? (Not literally in the building. In the metaphorical building.) A company-wide meeting was held and apparently it was . . . a lot. Much wailing and moaning and trauma dumping. From the site Choosingtherapy.com:

> Trauma dumping is an unhealthy behavior that tends to involve long, uninterrupted venting sessions about one or more stressful, painful, or traumatic experiences a person has

> had. One can do this to friends, family, or even colleagues and acquaintances, usually without others' full permission or consent . . . In the short term, this kind of excessive venting can provide relief to the person sharing.[34]

I wasn't there, but apparently at that meeting, and subsequent meetings, some serious dumping occurred. If I sound dismissive of the emotions on display in such a meeting, it's because I partially *am* dismissive. Partially.

I believe deeply in trauma; I believe people carry traumatic events with them. And I believe the pervasive pain of trauma is entirely real and can manifest in unexpected ways, ways we are only beginning to accept and learn from as a culture.

But I also believe there's something more going on here.

As days went by, a professional healer or counselor was brought in, more meetings were held, and more attempts at repair were made. With little success.

On the subject of me, the staff didn't budge. Not one of them would acknowledge that they might be wrong about me. Or even that the possibility existed that they could be wrong. Not one would agree there could be another way other than intransigence over my involvement. Some expressed outrage over even being made to consider these possibilities.

This intransigence is now quite common when companies are dealing with issues of sexism and racism. There is no flexibility: the perpetrator is wrong and possibly very evil, and there can only be condemnation for any act that potentially caused hurt. Intentions, as I said elsewhere, do not matter. The triggering and outrage are entirely justified.

When assholes argue online, they often refer to triggered, outraged people as snowflakes and accuse them of massive oversensitivity. I think this label is entirely wrong. They aren't snowflakes, they're survivors. Not survivors in the sense they survived trauma, but survivors in that they are staying alive in a system designed to trip people up. They are joining in and participating. It's the safe move to be outraged, to show your pain, to throw yourself on the side of the aggrieved. When you do, you are sticking with the herd.

If you aren't expressing pain and outrage, that means you place your happiness higher in importance than correcting the social ills of the world, and maybe that makes *you* the monster.

This is the world Gen Z has grown up in, a world where a massive chunk of who you are lives online, where it can be judged, attacked, and cancelled. Of *course* the smart thing to do is join in. And perform.

The ultimate case of joining in and performing came during a totally bizarre and insane moment in 1937. Stalin was ruling the Soviet Union with such a tight fist that anyone who crossed, or could cross him, or seemed that they might cross him, would be killed or imprisoned. In such an environment the safe move was to join in and perform.

That year, Stalin gave a speech to the Communist Party. When it was over, everyone applauded. And not just applauded, they went for it. Standing ovation, wild cheering, the works.

Which isn't so weird until you learn that applause went on for eleven minutes.

Try it. Stand up and clap for eleven minutes. It's exhausting. Now remember that many of the men clapping were very old and tired, most were war veterans, and some were very sick and infirm. And now add a further consideration: clap knowing that if you are the first to stop you will be cancelled. Cancelled Soviet-style.

The second-in-command could have stopped. But he was new and had just replaced a guy who had been thrown in jail for some infraction. Stalin could have stopped, but who can guess what went on in that sociopathic mind?

Finally, the director of a paper factory ceased clapping and sat down. Immediately everyone else did, too. They were saved! But that paper factory guy? Arrested and sent away for ten years. His interrogator was literally quoted advising, "never be the first to stop clapping."

I submit that meetings where people trauma dump in front of an audience to prove how committed they are to bleeding for some causes, while demonizing others', are using the allegiance to that cause as a kind of protective shield. Imagine if they had a sense of open-mindedness toward me when it got out that their company had employed me. They would all be the ones who sat down first. And everyone on Fishbowl would know it. Don't challenge a prevailing orthodoxy; applaud along with it. Affirm the pain and denounce the enemy and keep your friends and salary.

A school principal in Toronto named Richard Bilkszto challenged the orthodoxy in a diversity and inclusion meeting when the moderator stated that Canada was more racist than the United States. This principal, who was not right-wing but was by all accounts a decent liberal, challenged this point of view. In response he was shamed, suspended, and cancelled, and he reportedly lost friends. The incident so humiliated him he never recovered and killed himself two years later.

He shouldn't have sat down.

The people in that company meeting might truly believe that I'm evil and that they are purging evil by refusing any conversation with me and refusing to extend any second chance to someone they've decided needs to stay away. But I suspect they too are afraid to sit down. Because their colleagues are watching, and if word of my employment got out, the Internet is watching. Better to clap. Loudly. They know this, having grown up under the merciless eye of social media.

Stalin's secret police would be *in awe* at the reach of social media, and how willing we all are to spy on each other. They would rightly be worried for their jobs, because in our world, the people are policing themselves.

Those cheering for Stalin? They weren't snowflakes. They were *vyzhivshie*, "survivors," who knew what needed to be done to survive. They were raised in harsh environments and then lived in an extremely murderous one where a misstep meant jail and death. They kept clapping to survive. I can't honestly fault anyone for trying to survive. Life is better when you're not under suspicion or accusation.

But let's be honest, they weren't cheering.

Stand by your past self.
You didn't know what you know now.
—Unknown

The Las Vegas Fiasco

"I can't wait for you to get here; you're going to be surprised by how much everyone will welcome you," said Barbara Levy, organizer of the London International Awards (LIA), an advertising seminar and festival bizarrely never held in London, but instead Las Vegas. She named it after London because ad people always find Brits cool.* We can go ahead and file her statement under "Things that proved to be wildly incorrect," along with "The motorcar will never catch on" and "Germany wouldn't dare invade Poland."

LIA was unique in that it was focused on getting young professionals to Las Vegas to attend speeches and panels by older, more established professionals.** LIA also hosted the judging session of an award show. It promised the young attendees that they would rub shoulders with all the famous creatives, and the event

* Advertising's obsession with Brits is alive and well still, even though Aussies and even Swedes sometimes give them a run. We love Brits despite their status as the world's number-one oppressor. Look at a map; there isn't anywhere the British didn't shit all over. But who cares, in a meeting their accents sound so cool.

** I wrote LIA's tagline, "Created for Creatives." Not my best, but pretty good. Three words, short, simple, and to the point, decent alliteration.

consistently delivered. Everyone mixed freely, and some great, lively conversations were always to be had. Also, it's Las Vegas, so it got a little wild, although from what I saw, never truly Las Vegas–level gross.

I was invited to speak in 2019, which would be my fifth appearance throughout the years, always to a very warm reception. I gave speeches about all sorts of things, even once speaking to the audience about my favorite comic book artist, Jack Kirby, and the lessons we can learn from his career.* The trick to connecting to the audience is to be positive about the future of the industry, no matter how messed up it seems. One year, the global CCO of DDB, Amir Kassaei, gave a speech about how fucked the industry is and *bombed* (sorry, Amir). I went on next and talked about how awesome it is and got voted best speech. Problem is, Amir made good points—points that young professionals didn't want to hear.

This time was, of course, very different for me. I wasn't going in as CCO of the hottest agency, I was going in as a man guilty of #MeToo crimes, and in the ad world that title fell somewhere between serial killer and Chernobyl Worker Who Needs a Hug.

But I had a few things going for me. One, a lot of my old friends would be there too, in the audience, cheering for me. I got more than a few texts saying, "Can't wait for you to get here!" To see friendly, supportive faces was going to be so nice.

Second, I was going to be talking to creatives. Well, mostly creatives. The young attendees were largely copywriters, art

* Jack Kirby was the main creative force behind so many great comic book creations: The X-Men, the Hulk, Iron Man, Captain America. He should be as famous as Walt Disney. Jack never stopped creating, even when companies screwed him over. His joy in making great work never wavered, even as he got more bitter about the business. I always made the point that no creative should ever lose this joy, even when the business side crushes you. Funny how I've had to live up to my own words.

directors, designers, associate creative directors, and new creative directors. My people. My tribe.* I was one of them.

Third, I had even been invited by a mentoring organization to give advice to young creatives while I was there. Yes! Woo-hoo! The world was normal again!

Fourth, I was writing the speech of my life. It was one that could save my life. It was about compassion, empathy, and understanding, and how we can apply these qualities to the workplace. A message I was convinced people would want to hear. And a message that would show *my* humanity. Reveal me not as a monster, but as a flawed human being who had reflected on his experience and come out better for it. I even rehearsed the speech for my therapist, who said it was great.

I flew in feeling a mixture of fear and excitement. I was back in with my tribe. I was with my people. In the hotel, I ran into old friends immediately. It was so great to be hugged and smiled at. I wasn't a monster! They were happy to see me! This was going to be great. I was going to give my speech, drink with everybody, and I would be at home again in my industry.

And then . . . worseness.

On the day of the speech, the room was packed. About two hundred people, although it could have been more, a mix of the young creatives and professionals and the older judges and speakers. I looked around and saw so many friendly faces.

Before I went on, there was a speech by Lara Logan, the journalist and on-air reporter who suffered a horrific attack in Egypt in 2011. She had been reporting on the resignation of the president, Hosni Mubarak, when a mob surrounded her and raped her. It

* We can't say "tribe" anymore. Apparently, it's racist, even though every human being on earth has tribal origins. It's a commonality that we all firmly share, yet it's being used as another word with which people can call each other out for using. Righteous! I'm going to keep doing it, though, because it's the best word.

was shockingly, horribly brutal. One of the worst crimes a human being can suffer. Lara was amazing when she spoke. She was open and candid about her experience. She also touched on other brutal realities in the world, like the town of Tenancingo, which is basically the child-prostitution capital of Mexico. Lara's speech touched on many of the same themes mine did: not rushing to judgement, having empathy for others even when it's extremely difficult, and the need for real communication and understanding. It was so similar to mine that I began to worry whether my speech would be too repetitive. But I took heart that the room was responding so well to her and what she was saying. I was going to say the same things!

Yeah, no.*

I was introduced by Ralph Van Djik, a very nice creative, who was extremely generous in his remarks, saying I was important to the industry, etcetera. Really nice. I took the stage to decent applause. I introduced myself and touched on some of the things I was going to speak about, and then said, "But first I want to address something. Have you all heard of Diet Madison Avenue?"

The room went cold as one lone (deep, male) voice that clearly spoke for everyone emphatically said, "Yes."

"OK." My mouth was dry. "I want to address what they said about me." I then proceeded to show the posts they had written about me on a large screen, specifying how each was a lie, or not about me but written to seem as if it were about me, or just completely made up. This was finally my chance to show the world

---

* A note before you read what happened next: I have obviously thought about this speech many times since. And that I shouldn't have given it. What would I have said instead? A no-holds-barred speech about what I really thought about advertising. What I love, what I hate, but most important, I should have made it *about advertising*. I should have given what I had left to give professionally, instead of making it about me. I, too, suffer from narcissism.

that the narrative created about me was *wrong.* In one post, they had written that I had a trail of HR complaints. Not true at all. In another, they said that I had attacked a woman in a stairwell. Not true at all. I shook while speaking, describing to the audience how these posts had ruined my life and shattered my career, and the relief that finally I could speak out against them. One by one, I openly, publicly, emphatically denied all of them. I thought I was finally setting the record straight.

Nope.

Apparently, this was too much for one young woman. She had sat through Lara's speech about horrific rape and child prostitution, but seeing the Diet Madison Avenue posts about me triggered her to the degree that she went into the bathroom and couldn't come out. I knew nothing about this as I blundered onward.

Having assumed I had set the record straight, I got to the meatier parts of the speech. I spoke a bit about volunteering for a prison outreach program called the Freedom to Choose Project and what I had seen and learned there. How going into women's prisons had opened my eyes to just how deep abuse runs in our world, and how important it is for society to wake up to that. No reaction.

Then I got into advertising. Advertising needed to be more communicative (we're the communications industry, for God's sake!). We needed more empathy when dealing with each other, instead of taking offense and attacking one another, giving each other the benefit of the doubt without involving HR and lawyers so readily. Let's stop being angry and instead be the happy, creative industry I loved! I added other things along the way: creative tips, observations on how to manage others empathetically, and other reliably effective and popular things I had always said in the past.

My closing was another one of those reliable things. I usually ended with remarks about how shaky the ad industry can be, referencing the latest disaster or layoff. Then I always said, "Don't ever give up. The ad industry needs believers who love it. It needs passionate warriors for creative ideas. It needs people to stick with it and keep it great." Curiously, this didn't land as well as it had in the past. And now I think I know why.

As Jimmy Smith, the founder of Amusement Park, told me, "I thought the speech was pretty good, then I looked around and saw half the room agreed and half the room was angry."

Question-and-answer time was stilted but open. I wasn't sure I had gotten anything across that I had wanted to. But still I thought I was the old me again, talking to fellow creatives and peers. One person asked questions about forgiveness, which I thought was great. Another person, a woman, suggested I work on a series of sexual harassment videos as a creative effort at penance. "Great idea!" I said. "Want to write it with me?" She laughed but shrank back. Nope.

Then Judy John,* a woman I have known for years, spoke up. "I want to push you on the 'E' in empathy because I think you need to understand that in the position of power you have, what you do and what you say has more [impact] than everyone else. I think there is a lack of awareness around a little comment, like what someone is wearing, that is uncomfortable." I said I agreed, but that the concern was somewhat in the abstract. We agreed to talk about it afterward.

I came down off the stage, eager to hear how it had gone down. And it was *not good.* I was told about the woman in the bathroom. I offered to help but was told that would only traumatize her more.

---

* Judy and I were on the board of the One Club together. We never really connected. I was loud, she was quiet. But again, I have a horribly misguided habit of assuming I am automatically somebody's friend because we share a seat around a table. In the business world, this is known as "being an idiot."

Traumatize her? I had done nothing to this person. I did not know this person.*

Three guys came up to talk, ad creatives who still lived in the universe that I used to live in. They wanted to talk about cool work and funny ads, and I loved them and appreciated them but couldn't concentrate at all. The bad energy circling around the room was growing. Heaving.

Barbara Levy took the stage to try to quiet the room. She said she believed everyone had a right to defend themselves, and that she should know, having been raped in the past. This immediately painted her as a defender of the patriarchy, pouring gasoline all over the fire I had lit. The crowd of young people was already furious at her for a strange reason, which would become the main focus of articles in the weeks after: Apparently, LIA had a rule that anyone attending the conference *had* to go to all the events or their flights would not be covered by the organization, or something like that. The rule, as later explained to me, had been put in place because the whole thing was held in Vegas. In years past, many attendees hadn't gone to events because, duh, there's Vegas, just

* Someone told me that she went out partying that night and had a great time. The other young attendees got her out on the dance floor and cheered her on as a hero. Cool. There's a term out there that sums her actions up: crybully. Here's a definition of a crybully from Rachel Puryear in worldclasshugs.com: "Most, if not all other people, have dealt with a crybully before. It's never fun—in fact, these are some of the most heinous and vicious people you can deal with, because at first they can appear so vulnerable and sympathetic. But make no mistake—they will take without remorse and give nothing back even when they easily could, and they will not show a shred of the empathy they demand from others. Why is the crybully so dangerous? Because crybullies exploit the most prosocial of human traits, such as compassion, empathy, a desire to alleviate the suffering of others, and so forth. Meanwhile, the crybullies themselves show none of these prosocial traits to others." Or, as Freddie deBoer puts it: "This is the modern hell of crybullying, the person who tells you that you're oppressing them while they're busy mashing your face into the asphalt."

beckoning to them. So, LIA appeased the agencies underwriting the attendance fees by putting that rule in.

But, oh lordy, was this twisted to paint a picture of poor, innocent young advertising employees being trapped in a room with me, unable to leave. Perfect for a narrative. A great example of "vindictive protectiveness," a practice that Wiktionary defines as "A tendency to protect people from perceived injury (such as criticism) by responding with hostility to whoever is held responsible for causing said injury." The articles and online comments looking for something to be mad at could ignore everything I'd said. Except for one generous *Ad Age* article, which accurately reported my denials and my emphasis on understanding and empathy, everything else focused on the scenario of innocent youngsters forced to listen to an evil man.

If I had known they "couldn't" leave, I would have offered to personally pay for the flights of anyone who had been subject to that policy. When I began speaking, I had expected a few people to walk out and had been happy when they didn't. Maybe they wanted to listen to what I had to say! I had even opened with, "Thank you all so much for choosing to stay . . ." The attendance thing was bullshit. LIA later said, of course, they would have waived it. But a narrative is a narrative, and it was a good one. And that became the main narrative.

Well, that, and a special little initiative by *Campaign*, an industry magazine I had written for in the past. They zeroed in on one line I said in the name of contrition, "I have made mistakes, I flirted, I got high, and I bought into the myth of the creative rock star" (a myth that publications like *Campaign* built up for years). It was my attempt to say that I had bought into the industry's bullshit along with everyone else, but *Campaign* took that line and ran with it, citing it as proof that I was the embodiment of it. They wrote *three* different articles about that one line and how the creative rockstar needed to die, and I was the one to die so that it could all be over and everyone would be happy. The absolute very definition of a scapegoat.

Judy and I spoke late that day. It was a long, deeply frustrating conversation that basically boiled down to me saying, "I didn't do those things; I have a right to defend myself," and her saying, "This is not the time or place, and no one wants to hear from a white man right now." This last sentence is verbatim because it has seared itself into my head. "No one wants to hear from a white man right now." It meant, "Nothing matters, you are fucked." I think Judy meant well, but her tone with me was one of condescending exasperation. I'll bet that, to her, I represented men she was just sick of dealing with.

The shit rolled on for days. A creative director from France named Lauren Haberfield wrote an article in *Ad Age* so disconnected from reality that it had nothing at all to do with me. The best line was, "His right to speak usurped a woman's right to be offended." Which is insane. What woman? What right? Why does one nullify another? What?

I'll let British actor Stephen Fry take this one:

"It's now very common to hear people say, 'I'm rather offended by that.' As if that gives them certain rights. It's actually nothing more than a whine. 'I find that offensive.' It has no meaning. It has no purpose. It has no reason to be respected as a phrase. 'I am offended by that.' Well, so fucking what?"*[35]

Except for the first *Ad Age* article, every article and online comment expressed offense about me. Offense and outrage. A *Campaign Brief* article written by one of the young attendees

* Lindy West has a take on this well-worn quote. "The implication is that 'offense' is a dishonest, manipulative way to overstate hurt feelings, an attempt to make a frailty of the offended into an aggression of the offender." But I don't think that's right. Fry's take means that being offended *adds nothing* to an argument. In the face of an offended sensibility, Fry is asking, "But what's your actual point?"

wouldn't even mention my name. The author was so disgusted she had refused to type the letters of my name.* It was a shitstorm. LIA took a ton of heat as well, being accused of trapping the attendees in a bait-and-switch while supporting an old white man over the vulnerable young professionals. Time's Up Advertising went after them hard, threatening LIA with a boycott.

This is how crazy this shitstorm was: Time's Up Advertising, a group composed entirely of female senior executives, threatened the only major award show that is 100 percent female-owned with a boycott. After grandstanding for a few more weeks, Time's Up Advertising promptly disbanded for lack of interest. Everyone had gotten their resume-building accolade out of it.**

No one spoke publicly in my defense. No one. During my speech, I had put my email up on the screen in the hopes of starting conversations, hearing from those I had hurt, and finding chances to help heal the rift. How naive. I didn't get any challenges or debates or clarification questions.*** I did receive over

---

* I read that as I woke up the next morning, stunned at how ungenerous and unforgiving her words were. Wilting under the light of my new role as the Most Hated Man in All of Advertising, I went down to breakfast and walked into the room where everyone was eating breakfast, I came face-to-face with her. I froze. She froze. I couldn't speak. She glared at me. Her friends glared at me. Finally, all I could say was "I'm so sorry." And walked away, feeling their eyes burn into the back of my old white male guilty head.

** My favorite very-feminist female creative director hates Time's Up Advertising. She says, "They did nothing, absolutely nothing. An attention grab. A resume builder. Useless."

*** I did receive one email from a person requesting an apology. Not a woman, a guy. A planner who was angry at me because I had once called him out in a meeting. He had written a terrible brief and as he presented it to the room, I asked, "Did you write this brief or did you cut and paste it from the Internet?" He said he had written it himself. "Then why did you change fonts so often?" He had neglected to reformat his blatant cut-and-paste job, and the various fonts from different sources were easily recognizable. The room laughed. Droga5 was a tough crowd in those days; you didn't fuck around. If you bullshitted people, they would *pounce* on you. I had asked for one hundred emails of unequivocal support. These people were baffled, disgusted, angry, and sad, but also incredibly kind. One person wrote, "in an industry where people give speeches about bravery, that was actually the bravest I have ever seen someone be." Which was nice, but it gave me way too much credit.

I wasn't trying to be brave. I thought I was going to be welcomed and heard by my tribe. I went to Vegas as a creative and left as an oppressor. I didn't think I was facing up to a hostile enemy, I thought I was going to find empathy and understanding among fellow creatives and old friends.

I know why the rallying cry at the end of my speech to "never give up" had received such a tepid response. I was speaking to a room of people who *wanted me to give up.*

I had tried to go home for support. But home wasn't home for me anymore.

---

the chance to apologize to women I had offended, and this guy leapt at the chance to make a #MeToo moment all about him. He had gotten the brief wrong again.

Power

MeToo: . . .
Ted: What?
MeToo: I'm still processing.
Ted: Processing what?
MeToo: How incredibly tone-deaf you were to take that stage and say what you said.
Ted: *Sigh.* Yes. Go ahead. Hit me again.
MeToo: No, but do you *see* it? Do you see what position you put the attendees in?
Ted: I didn't think I was putting them in any "position."
MeToo: But you did.
Ted: Well, doesn't this just sum up *everything.* I unintentionally hurt people. Got cancelled. Tried to explain and defend myself, unintentionally "hurt" people again, got blamed for it, and got re-cancelled?
MeToo: Why did you put "hurt" in quotes?
Ted: What?
MeToo: You put hurt in quotes. Don't you think it actually hurt? Don't you understand that you can actually hurt people?
Ted: Yes, I know I am capable of hurting people. Do I think adults sitting in a room listening to a man defend himself is

hurting anyone? No, I have a hard time with that one. That kind of hurt is a power grab, a righteous rush disguised as pain.

MeToo: That is *so* not for you to say. You went into a room of happy, hopeful young professionals and ambushed them with your need for attention. They didn't want to hear that. They didn't know what you were going to say. What could make you think they wanted to listen to you defend yourself? Just sitting in that audience *is* an endorsement of you, and you forced them to endorse you by listening.

Ted: This attitude of "listening is endorsing" is frighteningly new. Kids didn't walk out of campus speeches until recently. The word "platforming" wasn't really used with as much gusto before 2016. I never thought I was gathering endorsements.

MeToo: That's bullshit. You went to Vegas to get endorsements.

Ted: No, I didn't.

MeToo: You went to Vegas to try and save your career.

Ted: OK. Partially. Yeah. I did.

MeToo: And inflicted your desperate desire on a group of people who *did not* sign up for it. Don't give me this "creative tribe" stuff. That's just something in your head. That's your narrative. And it's gone. You represent something else bigger in the world. The #MeToo movement dwarfs any concerns about creativity or ad people getting along and singing "kumbaya." You call yourself a scapegoat and then refuse to see how all-encompassing that role is.

Ted: I know. You're right. I wish I hadn't gone. It did make everything so much worse. You haven't really lived until someone from the other side of the world, whom you've never met, publishes an article calling you a monster, knowing you can say absolutely nothing to change that person's mind, set the record straight, or stop hundreds of people from believing her.

MeToo: You don't feel believed.

Ted: No, I don't! No one believes me or listens to me!

MeToo: WELCOME. TO. THE. CLUB.

Ted: OK, but is that the point? To make a man feel as bad as or worse than a woman does when no one believes her? This reframes the Vegas speech into something like performance art that everyone can be part of. Kind of a weird dance where the audience knows I want something and I know they want something, but really, it's a struggle over who's going to walk out of the room with the power.

MeToo: It's always been about power.

Ted: Yeah. Boy, am I thrown by this whole power thing. All I wanted was to be back in a space with my creative tribe.

A Space to Safely Fuck Up

Oh my God, New York can talk
Somewhere in all that talk is all the answers
Everybody owns the greats' ideas
And it feels like there's a big one' round the corner.

—ELBOW, "NEW YORK MORNING"

How great is it when the perfect song appears in the perfect moment of your life? When lyrics and life are in perfect sync? That's "New York Morning" by Elbow* and me walking into the offices of Droga5 on a late spring day in 2014. Elbow's song is about the amazing energy New York has, where anything can happen, and ideas are flying around to grab out of the air.

Droga5 had been up and running for six years, and we were humming on all levels. Every account was interesting and exciting, and

* Elbow is the best rock band you probably don't know. Like The Kinks, their hyper-Englishness is probably what kept them from breaking through in America. And the fact that their songs aren't about empowerment or how awesome you can be. Songs tackle complicated relationships, sadness, and tragedy. But put on "One Day Like This" on the first sunny day of spring and you will see.

every brief was a swing-for-the-fences moment. Even Prudential. When we won the Prudential account, people told us, "Ha! Now you'll have to do boring work." But the work we did for that client was great, interesting, and challenging.

"There's a big idea right around the corner." Is there a more electric feeling than that? Knowing that today you'll put your head together with some of the funniest, smartest people you've ever met, and a creative idea that didn't exist will be born. Soon! Today! It's enough to make even the walk to work crackle with energy and anticipation.

We had built a raucous, wild environment. The creative floor, in fact every floor, was *loud.* Laughter was everywhere. It was competitive in the best way, embodied by people like Cam Blackley, who, as I mentioned before, would work on briefs he wasn't even assigned to and drop the ideas on people's desks in the spirit of generosity (with a bit of "If you don't crack it, I will" competitiveness thrown in). It was generous: you helped someone out because a win for one was a win for everyone. We were a pirate ship against the world. Our Glassdoor ratings were through the roof. No one quit.

This spirit was embodied in the weirdest, happiest way: for no reason, at any time, people would break out in spontaneous whooping and cheering. Cries of "We did it!" would rise up above the cheers. What did we do? Nothing in particular. It was a completely stupid, silly, untethered expression of that same crackling energy.

And, importantly, people weren't afraid of each other and weren't afraid of saying the wrong thing.

Ideas need safe spaces. Ideas need the freedom to fuck up massively. Which means that sometimes someone is going to say something that someone else finds offensive. Barring anything obviously outright horrible, creative spaces should have the freedom to speak freely. Right now, anyone can read about Hollywood writers' rooms where people working on comedies are terrified to make the wrong kind of joke. Free debate in college classrooms seems as quaintly anachronistic as landlines and fax machines.

OK, yes, I am old. And I've been kicked out of advertising. But I love it, care for it, and want the wonderful things about it not to perish. And because I have the experience of it, I can remember when advertising creative spaces were unfettered and vital. Talk to anyone who worked at Wieden Portland in the '90s. The Nike ads, the highest of high industry standards, the work always being surprising and great, it was all amazing. The atmosphere was focused on doing work so creative it impressed and scared your peers. Is Wieden Portland doing better work today? Wieden leads the industry with inclusion efforts, and that is great. They don't just pay lip-service to inclusion, they fucking mean it. But can anyone say the work coming out of Wieden these days is as creatively vital as the body of work produced in the '90s? This is not a dig, it's a real question.

The two things don't have to be mutually exclusive. There has to be a way to create a safe space for people that is *also* a safe space for ideas. There has to be. Otherwise, what's the point of being a creative in an increasingly robotic industry?

As I wrote this, there was a crisis-of-the-week happening at a big agency. During an all-day cultural seminar, a CCO absent-mindedly sent a message to the whole group on Zoom: "This is fucking boring." He got skewered. And called a racist. Which was possibly the worst thing you could have been called in 2023.

Guess what? All-day meetings are boring, no matter what the subject is. I love the Beatles. I could talk anyone's ear off about the Beatles. But an all-day meeting about the Beatles would be boring as hell. I have no idea what was in this guy's head, but I can safely guess, as a high ranking creative in the advertising industry, he was far from racist and doing his best. Yet people online called for him to be fired.

This just in: As I write this, at another agency just last week a creative made a joke someone didn't like. This person was hauled in front of HR. Punishment is pending. We all have seen, firsthand, stories like this play out. Everyone in advertising is trying their best. Advertising, like anywhere else, is full of well-meaning people who occasionally fuck up. The point is they are well-meaning.

Punishing people for saying the "wrong" thing is not safety. It's cruelty of the kind that Aldous Huxley warned us of. And it's shutting down the freedom to fail, the freedom to fuck up, the freedom to fall down and get back up. We need failure to create. Creativity needs fuck ups. That freedom to fuck up is built with generosity, a generous notion that the person next to you is not mean and not evil, but a person worthy of compassion and understanding.

On my first day as an art director at my very first agency, an incredible thing happened. I showed up, met everyone, sat in my office awhile, and then just wandered around like the lost dork that I was. Everyone was kind and welcoming, but it was all a little stiff. So, a creative director called me into her office. She was so nice and chatty, but also aware of how hilariously awkward one's first day could be. As we chatted, a few other creatives stopped in. Here, I'll bet they were thinking, was a chance to size up the new guy. So, one of them tells a joke. It wasn't just a joke, it was one of those "that's really wrong" jokes. Everyone laughed and looked at me to see if I was laughing. I was.

Then we all really revved it up. We went around unloading the most awful, politically incorrect, absolutely-unable-to-be-repeated-here jokes we knew. And we were *crying* laughing. It became a contest of who could deliver the setups and punchlines with the most creativity and style, who could word them the best, who knew when to pause and when to drop the bomb. And again, the result was crying laughter.

OK, a few things:

First, it was immediately understood by all that telling the jokes was in *no way at all an endorsement of the content of these jokes or the actions performed in them*. This was not some secret society of evil people happy to meet like-minded monsters. Second, I realize this event occurred in a totally bygone era and I do not recommend or endorse in any way anyone doing this today. It's a recipe for HR to swoop in, behead you, and toss your carcass in the back dumpster. Third, yes, it was boundary pushing, but (at least to me and I know I can't speak for anyone else) it was done *not* with the intent to cross anyone's boundaries. Participants included men and women, aged between maybe twenty-five to sixty, and everyone was on a roll. Were some people offended by certain jokes? I would guess yes, but I would also guess the offense paled in comparison to what was actually happening. We were bonding. Not bonding over offensive material. Bonding over identifying ourselves as a group of people who could take risks together, creatively go anywhere together, and trust one another. Not in a "will you report me to HR?" way, but in a "will you venture with me to our creative boundaries?" sense.

Also, it was the declaration of a mission. And that mission was, "we are going to take every opportunity to make each other spit-take with laughter as often as possible." And man, did we all live up to that mission. Every day at that agency was a day filled with ridiculous, intelligent, inventive humor. And there was no fear of saying the wrong thing. I felt I was in the right place at the right time. And I think everyone in that room felt the same way. I asked most of them, and they do.

Miles Davis said, "It's not the note you play that's the wrong note—it's the note you play afterward that makes it right or wrong." How wonderful. Roll with it and turn it into something better. Why waste energy condemning someone for a wrong note, when that wrong note can lead to something so much better? In a way, Davis is getting selfish here, too, letting someone off the hook for an offense that might lead to an awesome creative moment for everyone involved. But why would you want to stifle a person when they may create brilliance *with* you, if you just let them be for a bit? This from a master of improvisation and creativity.

Go ahead and "OK Boomer" me (even though I am firmly Gen X). But I am most definitely not alone in this longing for a safe creative space. Ask anyone over the age of forty-five in advertising—or any creative field for that matter—and they will all have that place, the place where the work was fun, outrageous, silly, and full of pranks and laughter. These were *good* places. Places people tried hard to get into. Places where people stayed long after work hours were officially over because it was a lot more fun than going home. Places where great, memorable work was created.

We have gained more safety in our workspaces. We have gained more empathy. We have gained more respectfulness toward one another. But what have we lost? I emphatically do not want to go back to a time when it was OK to harass, intimidate, or hurt anyone. And yet I do believe that there is a way to regain the fun. I don't know anybody who feels like they have a space to safely be outrageous in.

Creativity is not a talent. It is a way of operating. And it's so much more fun for everyone when we know we are mutually safe to fuck up together.

John Cleese,* one of the creators of *Monty Python* and *Faulty Towers*, said it best in an interview:

---

* More English people. I love English music and humor. Cleese has complained about cancel culture for some time now, while avoiding cancellation easily. He's routinely denounced as an entitled white man who's been able to say anything he wants for a long time and should now be "held accountable." Say what you want about him, but the man produced some of the best comedy of the twentieth century. He knows creativity.

> The essence of playfulness is an openness to anything that may happen. The feeling that whatever happens is OK. So you cannot be playful if you're frightened that moving in some direction will be wrong. Something you shouldn't have done. Either you're free to play or you're not. As Alan Watts puts it, "You can't be spontaneous within reason." So you've got to risk saying things that are silly and illogical and wrong, and the best way to get the confidence to do that is to know that while you're being creative nothing is wrong. There's no such thing as a mistake, and any drivel may lead to the breakthrough.[36]

We can't be so scared as to not walk around the corner; that's where the big idea lives.

Droga5

The ideal man bears the accidents of life with dignity and grace, making the best of circumstances.

—ARISTOTLE

Search the internet for quotes about people letting you down, and you will be flooded with them. Quotes about how you need to remove people who have disappointed you from your life, quotes about thanking people for showing you who they are, quotes about moving on to something better—etc. etc. etc. An endless supply of sound bites and catchphrases and trite wisdom about how everyone else sucks and you should understand how much they suck as you pack it all up and walk away from them forever.

Search for quotes about *yourself* letting someone else down, and you won't find much at all. We live in a crazy, narcissistic world, where no one wants to acknowledge they've been the bad guy, and certainly no one wants to read about their own potential horribleness on some Pinterest board. Here's Noam Chomsky: "There are very few people who are going to look into the mirror and say, 'That person I see is a savage monster,' instead, they make up some construction that justifies what they do."[37]

I let Droga5 down.

I can't say much about Droga5, because I don't want to get sued. They made it clear that they would sue the fuck out of me, but that's just what companies do. They look after themselves. But writing and reading and rereading that last chapter brings me nothing but love for that place and what it was. Droga5 was my space to safely fuck up, my tribe, my home. I know that when firing me they were all acting in the best interests of themselves and the company. I understand that now. My love for who that group was and what we stood for has brought me to that understanding. That sad, shameful understanding: I let them down. I made our work vulnerable. They had to get rid of me.

That's all. I let you all down, and I'm sorry.

I decided I can't pay a person to rewind time,
so I may as well get over it.
—Serena Williams

Dropping the Rock

For the longest time I was planning to write a chapter about defensiveness, with a cloyingly clever title like "In Defense of Defensiveness" or something. It was going to be about how I felt when men tried to defend themselves during #MeToo, and they were told to not be defensive, and about how everything I wrote at the time was deemed defensive by my friends, advisors, and confidants. I was going to note that in many other situations a man can defend himself but not this one. I was going to get clever by comparing being defensive about #MeToo to being called defensive in a relationship, because that's really the space where defensiveness doesn't help and isn't constructive, and I was going to ask, why *doesn't* #MeToo conform to relationship rules?

At one point I was going to rant, really let loose, vomit it up, sometimes in aggressive ALL CAPS, everything that I want to say in my defense. Defensiveness is anger, isn't it? Buddha had a good saying about anger: "Anger is like grasping a hot rock with the intent of throwing it at someone else. But you are the only one who gets burned." Sing it, Buddha.

But, oh man, I'm tired of being defensive. I'm tired of fighting, even (and especially) with myself and the voices in my own head. I'm trying to be better. I really am. So, what I wrote before is out and this moment here is in. I've defended myself for much of this book already, but this is about the journey of wrestling with these big scary themes. Dealing with the anger and pain is only part of it.

This is where the tone shifts. Defensiveness doesn't help me, and it doesn't help anyone. I'm standing up, palms facing out, looking up at Buddha or whomever is listening, surrendering to it all, and preparing to be grateful for whatever comes.

I'm dropping the rock. There's some resistance from the hand that's been holding it all this time. I have to frantically wave my hand, unclench my fingers, so it will fall. But I swear I'm dropping it. Fuck off, rock.

Croisette Phonies and Old White Dudes

"Fuck you. Your family isn't happy. You're a sexual harasser."

I received this comment on an Instagram post while watching my son's basketball game on a chilly spring Sunday. His team was winning, and believe me, they don't always win. My son, in particular, was playing great. Some of the other dads and I were celebrating, happy our boys weren't getting crushed as usual.

I took a moment to look down at my phone and saw this new comment on a picture of my family at Christmas. The caption I'd written read, "Happy little family." A person I will call Alex, and don't know well, but well enough to have become an Insta-friend, had written the above.

Over the next few minutes, Alex's comments began appearing under other pictures.

"Fuck you. You are a monster."

"I pity your children, their father is a sexual harasser."

"Your life is a lie."

I froze with fear. I felt that familiar warmth rising from my stomach up to my face and head. I deleted the comments as quickly as they were coming in. And I wrote directly to Alex. All the while smiling to the people around me and pretending to know what was going on with the game.

Here is our conversation, verbatim. Typos also verbatim.

Me: Hello, Alex, that was an extraordinarily aggressive thing to write. Can we talk about it?

Alex: Nope. Welcome to the future.

Me: OK, I hear you, I just want you to know that we have been through an extraordinary amount of pain, and "the future" can and should be one of empathy and understanding. So my door is open any time to hear your perspective and your pain.

Alex: Fuck u

Me: I'm sorry that is your response.

Alex: God bless

And bonne chance

NRN

Me: I seriously would prefer to meet and talk. I truly believe empathy, understanding and communication are the way forward. I promise it will be productive. And I'm sorry for the way you feel. I don't believe I did anything to you personally and understand we live in quite painful times. Again my door is always open.

Alex: Dude. Old white dudr

This is MLK weekend

Stop

(It's at this point I realize Alex is probably drunk.)

Me: I'm also a parent, and a human being trying to make it in the world. Yes I am white, I cannot change that.

Alex: Get the fuck off my lawn.

(This is after Alex posted comments under my family photos. It's like crossing the street, trampling my flowers, and yelling "get off my lawn!" into my ring camera.)

Me: Let's get off each other's lawns. And maybe see if we can understand each other.

Alex: Unless you are_Actually doing useful things and leading—for the rest of which BTW is many of us. Yea agree.

(Also, it may be worth noting that Alex is in the C-suite of a major corporation. But I swallowed hard my desire to point that out and carried on, because "yea agree"! A sign of hope in the conversation!)

Me: Yes! I am. I am volunteering and working with a few groups. It's hard because many just outright say no. But if you know any other ways I can help I would LOVE to talk!

Alex: So please don't post bs "family" posts

(Something strange happened. I switched. I wasn't mad anymore. And I wasn't scared. Alex was in pain. I always talk about empathy, and yeah, you can practice it, but when it really hits it feels like nothing else. It feels good.)

Me: Well, it is Instagram and it is for friends. And I do love my family. As a parent you can understand that. I'm not trying to say that we are perfect, and I do want you to know that we have been very sad these past few years. So in no way am I saying all is good. Instagram doesn't paint an honest picture of reality. Family can be really hard. But I am totally for real about this. I would love to buy you a coffee and hear your story and perspective. After getting fired I met with dozens of people, mostly women, and listened to their stories about the industry, men, and the impact I may have had with them. I swear to you I am a very changed person. I know we live in an age that says intent doesn't matter, only impact. But I swear I never intended to cause hurt. But I did, I must have! Even though I still don't know who, because everything said about me was anonymous, I know enough to feel extraordinary remorse, guilt that I will carry a lifetime, but also a real desire to help change what I have caused or been a part of.

(Here I should note that when being genuinely earnest, I use the word "extraordinary" a lot.)

Alex: Every family on the planet has been very "sad" these past years and not been able to "tough it out" in million-dollar homes freelancing and having important thoughts -

(And here Alex went on a bit about a prominent ad person who defends and covers up for predators; I won't repeat it. But the resentment was striking and I understood Alex's motivations a bit more. Alex seems to have been through what a lot of people have: years, maybe decades, of resentment toward others who seem to have it easier or enjoy more advantages. It's worth mentioning the prominent ad person is someone I know well who is talented and works extremely hard. It's all so tangled and confusing.)

Alex: I believe what you claim so let's see how you use your position to champion "others" which TBH is actually the most of the rest of us—so I say this—if we see you boring old out of touch white elders posting about stuff you have no idea about and then showing up at yacht parties and making the same—old—vastly inappropriate jokes about the mother/daughter sex workers on the Croisette—well then I rest my case.

(Alex is referring to a mother-daughter prostitute pair who show up every year at The Cannes Lions International Festival of Creativity in June. They wear distinctive leopard print patterns and, Alex is right, draw a lot of comments and inappropriate jokes. Cannes, if I didn't explain before, is the very glamorous industry event that lasts for a week in the south of France. Besides ad professionals, a number of prostitutes walk the ocean front where the main hotels are, hoping to entice drunk ad people. However, Alex attends every year, so it's a little strange for her to be railing against my privilege. I think a lot of ad people struggle with their privilege; it's why they constantly make projects that are "doing good," either charity work or getting clients to take social justice positions publicly. This kind of work usually leads to more awards at the Cannes Lions International Festival of Creativity and more privilege. I did this too, felt gross about it, but went on stage and soaked up the applause.)

Alex: Try instead to make a better future for your and all the kids who, let's be honest, know and hate advertising.

And HNY! Let's never do this again!

(At this point, Alex then sent an article I wrote years ago, called "I Want to Marry a Producer." She provided no context.)

Me: Instead I married a creative and we are both pretty bad at planning anything.

Alex: Dude I wish you well.

Just make a better tomorrow for all of us

See you on the croisette and don't be a phony

A beintot

Me: Well, Alex, thank you for writing that, I wish you well too. But I don't think I'll ever be at Cannes again. Cannes is no longer an option for me, and I'm OK with that.

(I am not OK with that. Cannes is great fun with literally hundreds of old friends from around the world. I miss it terribly.)

Alex: Here's to a better tomorrow for the next generation an the planet—we did a shit job mostly, as stewards for the next generation—please be the human your 16 YO self believed

(That's a bad idea.)

Alex:—enjoy the days and years while we yet have them to share.

Me: Hear hear! And my invitation always stands, coffee and lots of listening to offer . . .

Alex: Copy that HNY

My god, what a relief. It had passed and we had come to a good place. What extraordinary (see?) validation for patience, empathy, communication, and working to understand. I was a mixture of real elation and lingering fear, fueled by the thought, *how many others are out there, ready to pounce on me like that?*

Whatever. I had applied everything I had learned and worked for and believed in since being fired and it worked. My ego had wanted to fight and defend, but I had put the ego aside. I'd had so many negative thoughts in the moments before that exchange got underway. A surge of my own righteous anger had made me consider cutting and pasting her comments into a message to her employer to get her fired. I had thought about calling my lawyer. But instead, I listened to Alex with empathy and tried to understand, and, I think, gained an actual friend? If we do see each other, I think we'll have that thing between us of having gone through this exchange together and come out the other side closer. I really believe that.

It's incredible, remove the ego and amazing things can happen. The ego wants to fight, but fighting almost never works. These days I take these small victories when I can get them.

Weeks later, Alex wrote again.

Alex: Thank you—for being gracious and forthright and generous and honest—it was truly misdirected trauma of my own having nothing to do with you — it was a hell of a year maybe someday we can all laugh about it but meanwhile and awkward know you have a friend and ally for life in me—see you round the way teddy and wishing and your family all the best.

Me: Fuck you asshole, you scared the living crap out of me.

Just kidding. I didn't write that. I was genuinely blown away. Alex didn't have to write that at all, but she showed real care and generosity in doing so. What a great note to get. I resolved to make this empathy and understanding thing work somehow, somewhere.

Since writing this I heard that Alex died. She passed suddenly and quite unexpectedly, at least that's what the rumor mill says. But I have learned to mistrust the rumor mill, so I don't know. I had and still have much larger-and-more-complex-than-expected feelings about this news. I have enormous gratitude for being able to connect with this person, go through the arc we did, and reach a point of, what would you call it, equilibrium?

At the same time, I also feel the starkness of how short and brutal life can be. Did she suffer? She was in some form of pain while she wrote to me, if I read between the lines of our exchanges. She, like all of us, was battling something, some inner demon, some struggle. Facing her own green monster in the cave.

Mostly I feel I want to hug everyone.

We're spinning toward our own endings, and it can all be over soon in a sudden *poof* of bad luck, a blocked artery, or a speeding bus.

Guys, everyone, can we all be friends again? We may not have much time left.

The Advance Fiasco

OK, now for a story about how I came to work at the worst place in all of marketing.* And in doing so I became embroiled in another workplace #MeToo drama. It's one that didn't involve me directly but did help me to experience the stress and pain involved from the other side in a way that was truly valuable.

The marketing world is weird. There are the top tier businesses, like great ad agencies and high-powered consultancies. Then there is a huge range of companies and individuals all peddling their particular expertise. Some are very good and driven by motivated, smart people. Some are lazy and rest on formulas. Some are a bit dodgy and will do or say whatever it takes to get clients (or more specifically, to get the client's money). There's a whole range of companies, from ethical to unethical, effective to scammy, happy to not-so-happy.

And then there's Advance.

* Advertising is one part of marketing. Marketing is figuring out what the customer needs, or thinks they need, even, and especially, if they don't need it. Advertising is telling the customer they need something, even and especially, when they don't need it.

If there's a bottom-feeder in the marketing world, Advance was nestled somewhere several feet below the worms living deep under that bottom. And after a twisted path back into employment, I found myself working for them.

I had started a digital agency under the umbrella of a small group that was putting together a PR firm, a design firm, and some small crypto players into an entity that seemed robust enough to take public. They had been looking to buy a digital agency, so my two partners and I said, "Don't do that, just set us up and we'll become your digital arm." And they said yes.

The network itself was ambitious, and yet strange. The people I met in the different divisions all seemed not to really know what was going on but were happy enough to go along with the plan to build a mini network. The guys putting the network together said all the right things, though they didn't really have strong agency backgrounds.

I didn't really mind. After being punched so hard in the face publicly, I just wanted to keep my head down and do work and get paid a salary. So, it seemed, did the rest of the network. The companies being mashed together were all small (thirty to fifty people), and all pretty decent at what they did. For a while it was fun. Nice folks, solid professionals. We won pitches together. And any problems we had seemed to be typical agency problems, politics, getting clients, arguments. I lunged at the normalcy of it all, starved for it, like an NYC rat lunges at a pizza crust.*

Besides its regular business, this mini network concentrated on making and selling NFTs, non-fungible tokens. I'm proud to say that from the beginning of the NFT craze it all smelled suspicious

* This line could be better; I'm workshopping it with some friends. The Pizza Rat thing is a placeholder. Options are (1) Like an underpaid junior creative lunges at an open bar, (2) Like a Brazilian ECD lunges at a Gold Lion, or (3) Like a CCO lunges at a podcast mic. We haven't nailed it yet.

to me, but I was also not smart enough to truly know or articulate why it all seemed so rotten. Yeah, yeah, crypto is the future, blah, blah, but it's *weird.* And the blockchain as a concept is cool but takes a half-hour to describe in a way that people understand, and once they do get it, they say, "Cool," and want to talk about *anything* else.

NFTs seemed to be all anyone wanted to talk about for about five months, so I went along with them because it's what clients wanted, and in advertising a big part of what we do, or what we are supposed to do, is give clients what they want. NFTs, after all, are just digital tools, and they did have some utility. They could provide membership, access, and personalized content. We had lots of meetings about NFTs. And they seemed interesting . . . I guess? At least that's what I kept saying to myself as people went crazy spending hundreds of thousands of dollars on badly illustrated cartoon-ape pictures.* The whole thing reminded me of a giant bubble I read about in school, the Dutch tulip craze of the 1600s.**

As the NFT and Metaverse mania went on and dreams of success danced in the heads of the C-suite, our little network bought Advance.

---

* The Bored Ape Yacht Club and all its imitators and extensions and whatevers will go down as one of the weirdest gold rush scams and deranged moments in financial history. Can't wait for the Adam McKay movie.

** From 1634 to 1637 the Dutch convinced themselves that tulips were amazing and would never lose value ever, because of course that's immediately what you would think about something that's a synonym for the word "delicate." Tulips traded for ever-more insane amounts of money for a couple years. One guy spent 100,000 florins on a tulip, when the average skilled worker made 250 florins a year. Then whatever they were smoking in their clay pipes wore off and the whole tulip market collapsed. Most contracts just weren't honored. This was before the blockchain, when you could still say, "Uh, no, I'm not going to pay that" and then not pay it. As far as I know, no one got murdered over tulips. Maybe they were all too embarrassed.

I will try my best to explain what Advance does, but I will do a bad job of it, I'm certain. We had been pushing this latest digital technology, but Advance was *waaay* behind on tech. As far as I could figure it out, Advance was a lead generation business, creating fake web pages and stress-inducing emails to get people to sign up for whatever service they were pushing, like legal services or hair care. If you've ever gotten an envelope with fake handwriting on it that says, "Hey, check this out!" or an email that says, "Payment due now!" when there is no payment due now, it could have been from Advance. Advance also set up web pages for clients that were fake competitors, so you could "shop and compare." No matter which you chose, you were really choosing their client. Basically, Advance tricked old, scared, and confused people.

It was loathsome and gross, and the CEO of Advance, because he acted most like he knew what he was doing, became the CEO of the whole mini network. If you've ever thought that business often boils down to whoever is bullshitting best, you're right. It really does. More often than anyone wants to admit. It's why American business seems specifically made for sociopaths to thrive. Bullshitters find rich hunting grounds, like hawks in New York City.*

This new CEO, Tinklepuss,** was a real piece of work. And by "work" I mean "shit." Tinklepuss could not *not* speak in business buzzwords every time he opened his mouth. He never said anything coherent, just bludgeoned everyone with dense-sounding nonsense until they nodded their heads to get him to stop. Tinklepuss called everyone an idiot behind their backs. Everyone.

---

* With its man-made canyons that make hovering easy and a super-liberal, rich populace that cares for them, New York is hawk paradise. Also, there is a huge amount of ready-to-eat meals in the form of rotund pigeons and pizza-crust-fattened rats. I knew the Pizza Rat thing would be handy somewhere.

** Not his real name.

Anytime someone left a room he would call that person an idiot to whoever was left in the room. This is an exact quote from Tinklepuss: "I'm a genius, and everyone else is an idiot." I hate the word toxic, because it is a word that is, in itself, toxic. It's a lazy word that people often use when they think something is bad but can't be bothered to really articulate why it's bad. But, man, Tinklepuss was *toxic*.

As most sociopaths are wont to do, Tinklepuss poured on the charm at the beginning of his time running the network. He even took my advice and hired two of the smartest, strongest, most competent women I have ever worked with to help run the network. Both quit within three weeks of getting to know Tinklepuss. Three weeks. You have to be uber-toxic to blow up a work relationship in three weeks.

If you ever met Tinklepuss, you'd quit after three weeks, too. Working with him was incredibly frustrating. As a creative person, I love clarity. I crave it. If you are clear with your mission and goals, then you can act with real purpose. But we were never clear with TP. Things were so unclear that I would often say to him, in the nicest way that I could, "I do not understand what you are saying or what you mean. You are being extremely unclear. You are speaking in business gobbledygook. The team does not know our goals or our mission. I think you are intentionally confusing us and possibly making this all up as you go." And he would call me and everyone else stupid, speak more gobbledygook, and leave.

Tinklepuss alone was not the only reason my friends quit. Because, you see, Tinklepuss had hired his mistress to be a senior executive for the network. And this mistress, Grendelpuss,* made Tinklepuss seem like the nice person. Grendelpuss inspired the two smart, strong, competent women I brought in to work there to take one look and say "nope" and leave immediately. She was

* Not her real name.

deeply threatened by other strong women, and my friends had lives that were too happy and full to waste battling Grendelpuss.

Here's a lovely example of Grendelpuss' charm and leadership skill: on the first day of work in January, Grendelpuss stood at the office elevator that opened into the lobby. She had an assistant with her, and she wrote down the exact time each employee showed up, mumbling something horrible and threatening to each of them. Then she never bothered to show up in the office again for the rest of the year.*

TP and GP wreaked havoc. They gave each other big bonuses whenever they could. They methodically froze out employee after employee, literally never communicating with them. I'm serious—they would not answer calls from *other CEOs of the network.* Then they began firing people and closing down each division of the network. First, they chopped off the crypto exchange (OK, fair enough). Then they cut off and closed down the PR firm (TP claimed it wasn't making money, but the firm had a decades-long history and a solid reputation). Then they wiped out the design firm that had been the heart of the network to begin with. It wasn't big, but it was good, and it built design systems that were complex, highly functional, and top-notch. Tinklepuss closed these divisions down mostly because he didn't understand how any business ran other than his own (and that, too, is in doubt). As for my division, Tinklepuss gutted it without any warning to me or my partners, retained four of us as Advance's creative department, and fired the rest.

If you're wondering why I didn't leave, I must remind you that at this point in my career I was still Ted Royer. And as Ted Royer I was fairly sure my job options in any sort of legitimate

* Except once in March, when she stormed into the office, yelled "Where is everybody!?" collected her yoga mat and left immediately. I am not making this up.

marketing-related field were below nil. This was helpfully confirmed by all the headhunters I had ever known and worked with for years, who had said, in unison, "No. No jobs for you. Even if you weren't Ted Royer, which you are, you're still an aging white man, and no one wants one of those anyway."*

So, stuck in it and scared, I soldiered on with my team. And here's where it got worse, but in a weird way for the journey of my soul, better.

When we were running the digital agency, I hired a project manager. Let's call her Elspeth.** Elspeth was fun and funny and a little crazy in a good, advertising-y way. She also was young and loved to go out drinking with coworkers. Elspeth joined Advance to work with me while the Great Destruction of Divisions was underway. Elspeth, being young and foolish and free-spirited, got herself involved with a guy at work. Let's call him Gunther.***

The relationship quickly turned, one might say, unhealthy. Let's further say that by any definition, she was sexually harassed. I saw some of the texts this guy sent her, and they weren't great. Let's even further say that Elspeth needed to untangle herself ASAP.

Untangle she tried, but things got worse. More alcohol was involved, more texts, and more not-great stuff. I don't know, nor is it my place to say, the details. It's not my story. But here's where it gets bad. Gunther was a protégé of Tinklepuss, and at this point he knew *all about* TP and GP, so it behooved them to keep Gunther happy or he could blow them up. And once TP and GP heard his relationship with Elspeth had gone south, they advised Gunther to go to HR first and report *her* as the harasser. Fun!

---

* This is a real quote, said over and over by real headhunters.

** Not her real name, but a name she chose for this story.

*** Not his real name, but funny to a few people for reasons you'll never know.

Long horrible story short, Elspeth got fired and Gunther kept his job.

Seeing this deeply fucked-up turn of events, I complained to HR. Not only about Elspeth's inexcusable treatment, but also about how fucking toxic (that word really is useful when it's accurate) TP and GP were to work for.

Then, after a few more weeks, I was fired.

I can't prove that it was retaliation, but it damn well felt like it. Two weeks before I was fired, the senior leaders of the company were asked to give presentations about its future. I gave mine on our creative vision for AI, and what we could build together with it in the coming months. I got a huge round of applause and the only "fucking awesome" shout-out of the day. I got emails from people I didn't know saying how excited they were to work with me. People stopped into my office to ask how we could do more together. But I got fired. The reason given was "didn't meet new business goals." Never mind that no business goal was ever articulated by TP or his underlings, and that my team and I had been searching for business by ourselves with no support or guidance at all, just occasional words to the effect of "hang tight, direction is coming soon." So no, I can't prove it was retaliation, but I'd bet my X-Men comic book collection it was.*

So, I wrote a letter. Or more accurately, a lawyer I hired wrote a letter. It detailed every single thing I knew about Tinklepuss and Grendelpuss, about what a shit show the company was, and how toxic and rudderless it had been. Unlike Droga5, this fight I wanted to fight.

But, most importantly, we detailed the shitty treatment Elspeth had received. And as I sent the letter, I marveled at the irony that Ted the monster had witnessed a woman being treated like it was 1980, and in his own small way raised a hand in her defense, even

* The complete John Byrne/Chris Claremont run. Yeah.

if it was too little, too late. And then I thought, maybe it's not so ironic at all; maybe this kind of shitty treatment really is everywhere, and I was blind to it. Insulated from it. And now it was a bit of a gift from the universe to see it up close from another angle.

Elspeth's story is the kind that I would have ignored before, or shrugged off as being frivolous or outside the norm. But this grenade had gone off right outside my door, and maybe that meant grenades were going off *all the time*, from the worst companies up to the rarefied, hyper-privileged world of advertising I had come from. Was this what the average office experience was like for the Elspeth's? #MeToo-type thinking clearly hadn't yet reached a prehistoric company like Advance; was this what the business world had been hiding all along? If so, it's pretty fucked up, and I felt even worse for having been a part of it at all on any level.

And TP and GP proved that a couple in power can be a *dangerous* thing. It was obvious to all that they were looking out only for each other and everyone else be damned. Their coupling created an alliance that left everyone on the outside but them. I'm not saying most or even some are that bad, but they can get bad in a way that's no one else's fault around them. As my old boss Ellis Verdi says, "Never hire a couple. Never, ever, ever. Ever." For everyone's sake and sanity, I really believe that work couples need to be a thing of the past. Banning dating between coworkers is antihuman and I especially don't love having a company dictate who we can and cannot date or fall in love with, but right now, at this time in the world, it's just not a good move.

There is something of a happy ending to the Advance fiasco. Two weeks after I sent my letter, Tinklepuss and Grendelpuss were both fired. They and Advance are currently suing the shit out of each other. Advance has since filed for bankruptcy, which is sad because there are some nice folks still there and I wish them well.

Elspeth and I are still friends and still working on projects together.

A Letter

It's hard to write this, because I'm afraid to take accountability. Being accountable in today's world is like picking up a shovel, smashing yourself over the head repeatedly and then burying yourself. People tell me all the time, "Never apologize, never." But this is a book about #MeToo and me and the world, and that means you too. And you deserve an apology. So here goes.

I'm writing this to you, the woman I've hurt. Or may have hurt. I don't know. I don't know if you were part of any of this. And I'm going to leave out any detail about you because you deserve to be safe from scrutiny or any adverse attention. I don't know how you feel about me now. I don't know whether you complained about me, and I don't need to know. That's not the point. The point is, I've reflected a lot on how you may have felt, and how my behavior may have impacted you.

I was attracted to you. I thought you were also attracted to me. But did you feel pressure to *act* as though you were attracted to me? If you did, that's awful. For my part, I really thought our attraction was mutual. I thought it really was. Maybe the drinks and the laughter made me blind. We drank together and laughed a lot. Did that make you uncomfortable? It seemed real, but that's not for me to say. My attraction to you, and the fact that we had fun, certainly blinded me to seeing anything else. That's my fault. Also, what does it really matter if our attraction was real? It *still* could have made you feel uncomfortable.

Throughout our time at work, I talked to you more than I did to others. I gave you more attention. I laughed with you in the hallway; I made a point to come visit your desk. Did that bring undue, unwanted attention to you? Not just from me but from your friends and coworkers? Did it open the door so others could gossip about you, let them ridicule you?

It's a horrible position to be put in; people could have accused you of all sorts of things. Forget me; from their point of view, how did *I* make *you* look to them? My selfish desire for attention opened the door for a whole list of judgements against you that you couldn't control. Oh my god, that was deeply unfair to you.

And I stupidly, stupidly never thought about power. The power I had putting you in the position that put you in. You could have said no, thank you. But could you have? And not been nervous doing so? You didn't know me well, you couldn't fully know how I might react. Women face retaliation *all the time*, why should you imagine I would be different? And then, later, when you did gently and tactfully push me away, I left the door open for something to happen between us. This was so selfish. Did that make you feel like I wouldn't go away? Did you feel pressure to keep responding? I'm so, so very sorry if it did.

I was stupid, and I was unsympathetic. I never thought nearly enough about the impact my attention could have on you, your career, and the people around you. They didn't need that weirdness. They didn't need to be in an office environment where a senior leader felt he could do that. I was stupid, I believed advertising was a permissive, flirtatious, hook-up environment. (And we know it was.) But it shouldn't have been. *I* shouldn't have been.

Not there, in that agency, or anywhere. That's my responsibility. I was and am accountable for that.

You were so sweet. You were delightful. You were my friend. I really cared about you. When we said goodbye, I felt genuine affection for you and wished you the best. You seemed to feel the same. Did you feel relieved to be away from me? That breaks my heart if you did.

Sometimes I would blunder around assuming that if I was having a great time, then everyone was having a great time. Clearly not everyone had a great time. The ad industry often told us to act young and to be childlike with our wonder and other dumb, obsessed-with-youth quotes. And I was childish, the bad kind of childish. I played like a child, unconcerned with the consequences that you might have felt.

I don't know if you complained about me, and I don't ever need to know. That's not the point. The point is I hope this reaches you, and if there's ever, *any* way I can make amends, I will. That door will always be open.

You didn't deserve to feel uncomfortable around me for one second.

If you did, I failed you. And I'm sorry.

Statler, Waldorf, and Skittles

In the last week of June, the elite of the ad community go off to the south of France for the Cannes Lions International Festival of Creativity. It's a great boondoggle; an excuse for ad execs to tell themselves they're crushing it, drink overpriced rosé, and circle jerk each other while wearing expensive linen. I used to love it. Seeing people I knew from all over the world, making new friends and contacts, usually picking up some awards that made me feel like I was on top of the world, and returning home with a killer tan and some great stories.

During the same week in 2020, instead of frolicking in France, I went to jail.

What I mean is that I volunteered with a group that visits maximum security prisons and talks to the inmates. It's called Freedom to Choose. Their mission is this: The Freedom to Choose Project (FTC) is all about redemption and the power of second chances. We assist men and women in stepping free of past identifications as "criminals" and reidentifying themselves as valuable members of our society.

FTC's goal is inspiringly noble. They seek to reduce prison violence and recidivism rates by going into prisons and working with the prisoners. They believe deeply that prisoners are capable of rehabilitation and change, and that change is a choice available to everyone. It is one's response to events that truly matters. Though you can't choose what happens in life, real freedom comes from choosing *how* you respond to it. Anger is a choice, revenge is a choice, love is a choice, what you choose to honor is a choice, and how you shape yourself is a choice. It's all about choices.

I wanted to work with FTC for a pretty obvious reason. The #MeToo movement was and is about women getting justice for being abused. Society needed to become aware of and change a culture of abuse toward women. So far, I had only heard from businesswomen and their #MeToo stories: being hit on at work was terrible, misogyny was pervasive, and men generally were loutish brutes at best and coercive power abusers at worst.

But there was so much worse out there. FTC goes into prisons to do their work, and from what I learned from their organization, women's prisons are filled with inmates who were often sexually abused at a very young age, almost always by men they trusted or depended on. The formula is simple: Get abused by a trusted figure, turn to drugs and alcohol to cover up or avoid the deep pain, fall into the wrong crowd, commit or become involved in a serious crime with said wrong crowd, and go to prison. As one deputy warden said to me, "If we somehow got rid of child abuse, this place would be 90 percent empty."

FTC treats both female and male prisoners as actual, equal, human beings (which is how they are almost never treated by the system). Committing a crime, and being imprisoned for it, devastates one's sense of self. According to the FTC, inmates imprison themselves in their minds as well as in a jail. They see themselves as worthless, dangerous, subhuman. FTC offers them a chance to connect with their humanity, and with that connection, find a way out of the nightmarish self-perceptions of a mind-made prison. It's beautiful, heady stuff.

We arrived at a Holiday Inn–level hotel in Anaheim in dry June heat. There were about fifty of us volunteers milling around, making small talk, and drinking terrible hotel coffee. It quickly became obvious that many of these people were returning, because there were warm hugs and smiling hellos among some. People were extremely nice, and very quiet, in that self-help kind of way, choosing their words for minimum offense or impact. Some were covered in a thick layer of hippie, wearing flowing clothes and homemade jewelry. Others carried the look and posture of people who have been through some serious shit, like abuse, alcohol, and drugs. You know, real-life calamities. I was slowly nurturing a newfound love for people who had been through serious shit, but at the time this love was just forming, and I still felt separate from it.

I was still wrestling with the type of shame people probably feel when going to rehab for the first time. And Shame threw doozies at me: *What are you doing here? Are you one of these people? I thought you were cool. You should be in Cannes on a yacht, sloshing wine on your linen shirt and high fiving a director, feeling great about your life choices.**

Shame echoed what my ad friends would have said: groups like FTC were made up of people who had failed and bottomed out. These people didn't have granite pools or speak at cutting-edge tech conferences. These people were losers.

And you're one of them, laughed Shame.

* I often thought about one moment in Cannes: a group of ad creatives had been flown, by a fleet of helicopters, to a secluded island where we lounged by an enormous pool, ate from enormous tables completely covered in sushi, and drank endless wine and champagne while standing and dancing in said swimming pool. At one point, someone looked at their phone and said, "Hey, the stock market is crashing!" And everyone laughed and kept dancing. It was both enormously entitled douche-baggery, but also very dark humor. It can be both things.

Shame settled in to watch the hippie show. We gathered in a hotel conference room for our orientation, where there was a lot of standing in circles, breathing exercises, and acknowledging each other. All afternoon and evening we did training sessions to understand better what working in the prison would be like. Rules were thoroughly run through; prisons are no joke, and following procedures was very important. The atmosphere was a mix of solemn purpose and true compassion. Flexibility was particularly stressed; an informal motto of FTC was "we are so-o-o flexible!"*
Because when you're dealing with prisons, things can change instantaneously. Overall, the mission was noble, and you could see that these kind folks were happy to be part of it.

I was, however, detecting a dash of performative, New Age–type communicating among the group, some "O-o-oh look at me, I care more than anyone" attitude. And, right on cue, Cynicism showed up, taking a seat next to Shame and together they became Statler and Waldorf from the Muppets. They settled into their theater box in my head to mock the proceedings together. Statler and Waldorf lobbed comments and insults at me as we ended the evening. We closed it with some group humming and some blessings, because of course we did. S&W howled with laughter.**

Driving to The California Institution for Women in Corona, California, the next day was intense. The prison is set out in the

* I'm happy to say I've brought this motto into my parenting. You know who aren't flexible? Children. They are hard core when it comes to schedules and expectations. Change something up and they lose their little minds. "We are so-o-o flexible" is an awesome family motto. Of course, my children weaponized it quickly. "Why can't we do what I want to do?" they now say, "I thought we were so-o-o flexible."

** FTC is very spiritual. Interestingly, the word "God" was almost never used. "Spirit" was invoked often. From what I could tell about this, God is a representation of organized religion and all its faults, whereas Spirit is more squishy, less defined, and therefore more personable and ownable by each individual.

middle of endless flat desert, where you can see for miles in every direction. It bakes under the sun, with totally oppressive, wavy heat blob distortions that shimmer on the horizon. The CA Institution is a series of large concrete buildings that house offenders from level 1 (low risk of repeat offense) to level 3 (high risk). These people have done, or been involved in, some serious shit. We were going to do our work with bank robbers and murderers. Many of these women would never see the outside world ever again.

There were lots of security checks, lines, and periods of waiting. No phones were allowed. We were shown through some large gates and barbed wire fences and into a courtyard, where we had our first glimpse of the inmates, and they of us. Most smiled, some glared. Finally, we shuffled into and settled in a cavernous meeting room with a ceiling three stories high. Imagine a high school gym in East Germany in 1970. We were seated in rows of plastic chairs and given more orientation training.

Then the inmates came in. They sat around and among us. This was intentional as we were meeting them on an equal, human level from the get-go. It was also a little disturbing, playing a game of "which one would murder me if she could?" in my head. The surreality was heightened by the internal efforts of my brain constantly telling my face not to show any signs of disturbance or fear. Also, inside my head, Statler and Waldorf were laughing and throwing popcorn at me while telling me how stupid my face looked with its fake, dumb smile. Then they asked if I was missing a glass of French rosé right about now. I was.

There were several speakers addressing our mixed group. The overarching theme of their remarks was about recognizing that thoughts create reality, so you could be "free" if you controlled your thoughts and used them to create the reality you truly wanted. Freedom comes from breaking the cycles inside our brains. Step outside your emotional, clouded thinking and recognize anger, negative self-perceptions, and addictive behaviors.

Don't cooperate with the negative thoughts and actions. For example, instead of thinking, "I'm a murderer," one could think, "Life and my actions placed me in the position where I committed murder, but that is not who I am. I am a person who can overcome my past and decide who I *really* am." Define yourself inside, and you can start to define your world outside. Inner reality creates outer reality. Thus, you can be "free" even while you're in prison.

We practiced this together by forming "trios." In each trio, one person would recognize a destructive pattern in themselves and tell a story that illustrated that pattern. This person was the sharer. The next person would ask nonjudgmental questions and make observations to draw out understanding and perspective from the sharer. This person was the facilitator. And the third person was the neutral observer, who didn't speak until the end, and whose purpose was to "hold space" for the other two. We were supposed to never react, only listen and reflect back to the sharer what we were hearing. We would switch roles in each trio until everyone had performed each role.

The day was great. Really amazing conversations with some awesome women. The inmates, by and large, were super-engaged in the process, hugely forthcoming with stories (some unbelievably tragic) and wonderfully empathetic to anyone else's story or situation. Statler, Waldorf, and I all expected I would be ridiculed for even mentioning my own white-boy- Philadelphia-Main-Line problems, and we were all wrong. The inmates *loved* talking about anything. It was easy to see it helped them feel normal.

My second favorite person of the day was Shirl, a woman in her sixties, wheelchair-bound, who had suffered horrific abuse from the men in her life from a very early age. Shirl had an amazing life force, even though she had every reason in the world to be bitter, angry, and hateful. She and I connected instantly and laughed a lot. Shirl was the embodiment of Freedom to Choose. FTC's philosophy is based on the work of Viktor Frankl, who famously survived the Holocaust by taking control of his inner reality. Shirl and Viktor would have been best buds. When we'd finished our trio, Shirl and I told each other we loved each other, and we meant it. In FTC, you cannot hug or shake hands, no touching is allowed, so what you do is cross your arms over your own chest in a self-hugging motion. Shirl and I self-hugged a bunch. Statler and Waldorf were quiet. They loved Shirl too. It's against the rules to stay in touch with the inmates, so, Shirl, if by chance you ever read this, I love you.

But the hands-down champion of the day was Skittles.* Skittles was about twenty-seven years old, thin, wiry, with short hair and a very high energy level. She had the presence and energy of someone who could go off at any moment and had to get up and leave our trio twice because she was overwhelmed with emotion. Skittles was a raw nerve, but also preternaturally in tune with people around her. She vibrated on a bunch of frequencies. She was a powerful antenna, receiving and sending out signals. Skittles was alive.

When it was Skittles' turn to be the sharer, she told a devastating story about loss and family, which I won't repeat because it's not mine to tell, but her openness was amazing and she presented her struggle completely unfiltered. We reflected the things we heard back to her, marveling at the strength she showed, and she was very grateful.

Then it was my turn to share a belief about myself and a story about the creation of that belief. I had used up my big guns in other trios, my #MeToo shame, my suicidal thoughts, and so with Skittles (and Jane, our other trio member) I reached deep and pulled out something that had flared up regularly my whole life though I'd rarely ever talked about it. It was a story about shame and about feeling like a loser, so Statler and Waldorf sat

* Obviously not her real name but in fact her real actual awesome nickname.

up straight, preparing to wail on me. They were ready to pile on shame and embarrassment because the story was about (1) suburban privileged upbringing, (2) private school, and (3) Dad being disappointed in me. No hitting, no yelling, no abuse, no killing. Nothing like the deep horrors these women had gone through. Just disappointment.

I had been getting terrible grades in physics at my high school. I studied hard and pulled out a 73 on my next test. I was happy about showing improvement and called my dad, who lived in a different house after my parents divorced, to tell him the good news.

Dad answered the phone. I told him my grade. Silence.

Then he said, "You're happy about that?"

It was my turn to be silent. I just listened. Tears welled up. I couldn't stop them. Dad could always make me cry.

"A 73. That's not even halfway to 100. That's *terrible*, and you're *happy about that?*"

I cried then, and in the prison, I began to cry again. I hated this memory. This moment was the last time I ever tried to impress my dad because fuck him. He died of cancer two years later and I would never try again. He had taken my proud moment and smashed it.

My mom, in the background, kept saying "Hang the phone up. Hang it up." But I wouldn't. I stood there listening. Now he could tell I was crying.

"Oh, you're crying?" he said, contemptuously. Yep, contempt. I could hear it clearly. "OK. Fine. 73 is good. Good for you. Congratulations."

"Thanks," I said, and hung up.

As I recounted this, Statler whispered in my ear, "You are such a pussy."

But Skittles wasn't thinking that at all. She was staring right at me listening to everything. "That is so sad," she said.

"I know, I felt terrible. I've felt awful about it ever since."

"No, not you." Skittles said.

"What?"

"Your dad. I feel so bad for him."

Bad for him? What the hell? This was a moment about *me.* I had been carrying this around deep in my psyche for decades. This had been a defining moment for me. My stupidity and wimpiness had been poured into concrete and set forever, and she felt bad for *him*?

"What do you mean?" I asked her.

"Well, think about it. He's all alone in his house. His wife is gone, his kids are gone. You told me he drank, right? He was probably drinking alone in his house, and his son calls, happy. Living life without him, moving forward without him, succeeding without him. And he had nothing to do with it. At that moment he probably felt so alone. He probably felt it had all slipped away from him. That you had slipped away from him. I think he was lashing out at you because of that. I feel really bad for him."

The moment she said it, in a flash, I could see it all like a movie scene. The orange light of the low, sinking afternoon sun coming in through my dad's den. The sunbeams illuminating the dust in the air around him. Dad sitting in his burgundy leather chair, glass of scotch in his hand. He looks like he is scowling at nothing. The phone is hung up next to him. And he's just sitting. Alone.

Jesus Christ, Skittles.

She'd just judo-flipped one of the worst memories of my life into a huge wave of love and empathy for my dad. I'd whipped up the familiar ancient anger during the storytelling, and it evaporated into thin air almost immediately. I wanted nothing more in that moment than to hug Dad. Statler and Waldorf got their coats and began to leave the theater.

I thanked Skittles many times. She laughed and said, "Of course," as if she did this twenty times a day, which she probably did. I cried. Skittles cried. Jane didn't cry. Have I mentioned

Jane? Jane was holding space as the facilitator. Jane was tough as hell. Jane didn't cry easily. She did point to Skittles and say, "Yeah. That's Skittles for ya."

I think Skittles did more for me at that one moment than any therapist I've ever had. Her raw, beautifully simple blurting out of the truth felt more real and less calculated than anything else I could have heard or thought. I still tell the story of how Skittles fixed my relationship with my dead dad. And I swear, since then I haven't had a bad thought about him.

I had gone into FTC to understand #MeToo and gotten something else as well in return. This wasn't just #MeToo, this was about connecting to all humans more compassionately. These women were more open, more generous, and more in touch with who they were than most people I'd encountered on the planet. Maybe they had to be in order to survive. But I don't know that I'd ever had a conversation as inspiring and honest as those that I had with total strangers who may or may not have killed someone. I left that prison and FTC thinking the work they were doing was work that everyone, everywhere, should be doing. Every high school, every college, every marriage, every office. It was cathartic, reality-shifting, mountain-moving stuff. Change your inner reality and you change everything. It all seemed so obvious yet had been so elusive. But most of us don't do it. Even now I have to practice it. What does that say about how we live on the outside? I don't know, I'm still working it out. But, damn.

My head was swimming as we stood outside the prison letting the experience settle in. Statler and Waldorf peeked back through the curtain. Then they got really excited to retake their seats, because the hippie contingent asked us all to hold hands and sing John Lennon's "Imagine."

Stadler and Waldorf opened their mouths to mock the singing, but I said, stop. Not today, guys. Not today.

And I sang.

To keep going, despite everything.
—Unknown

The Universe and, Like, Oneness and Everything

My life was taking on some dimension again—some professional work, *the work*, some rebuilding of a normal-ish life—and yet, the pain still sucked. The relentless thoughts still sucked. The banishment still sucked. The unending self-judgement still sucked. It had been four years of feeling like shit and thinking like shit and I was up for some drastic action. I knew what I needed: more drugs!

I got a recommendation to see a woman in San Diego named Ginger who ran her own practice offering a combined DMT and psilocybin treatment. The idea is that these powerful substances can literally disrupt your thought patterns by getting your brain's record needle to jump out of the groove in which it's stuck. Sounded good to me. Plus, tripping is always powerful, and having a guide to make it more therapeutic sounded great.

I fasted for twenty-four hours, didn't have alcohol during the week prior, and tried to eat healthfully to get my body ready. I say tried, because burritos.

I flew to San Diego and drove a rental car to Ginger's home in a nice suburb, where she answered the door with a bright

"Hello!" She was in her early forties, bubbly, and very kind. She had a Southern California lilt to her voice, almost Valley girl but not quite. She didn't say "like" and "totally" a lot, but her voice *sounded* like she was saying "like" and "totally." I'm not judging. Ginger was incredibly nice and welcoming and fun to talk to. I only bring up her distinct, SoCal voice because during the intense cosmic journey, having a Valley-girl-esque voice keeping you from getting lost in the void was, well, a little incongruous. If I were writing this as a movie scene, let's just say her voice would have been a debatable creative choice.

Ginger showed me her garden, which stretched around the side of her house to the backyard. Of course, she was "super" into plants and flowers. Isn't everybody who's spiritual into plants? It would actually be refreshing to find a shaman or guru who thought taking care of plants was a pain in the ass because it cut into their TV-watching time.

We went inside Ginger's spacious, sunlit home. Up a small flight of stairs was her studio, a very bright space with a low ceiling and windows on three sides. There was soft, white wall-to-wall carpeting, huge throw pillows everywhere, Eastern-style decorations, Tibetan thangkas, and Buddha statues. And of course, more plants. There were no hard surfaces or sharp edges. In the center of the room was a low, tatami-like mat that seemed much bigger than king size, but that may have been because of its central position. I was instructed to sit down. This mat would be my home, my cocoon, and universe-traversing spaceship for the next several hours.

We talked for about an hour, about life, about pain, about the brain and how it works, about relationships, about a lot of stuff. She told me about the work she does with many different people, from combat veterans who are dealing with battlefield trauma to rich Hollywood executives who are wondering if this is all there is to life. I said I had huge sympathy for the former and almost none for the latter. Ginger patiently reminded me that everyone's pain is relative, that maybe I could acknowledge I was way closer to the self-involved movie executive than I was to the combat veteran on the pain scale, and that my instant lack of sympathy reflected my own self-hating problem. She didn't say that last part out loud, but I think she knew our conversation could steer me toward that understanding. Realization of my self-involvement and self-loathing? We were off to a roaring start.

She also explained that during the DMT/psilocybin experience people in her care had reacted in pretty much any way you could imagine. Screaming, crying, throwing up, wetting themselves. Some thrashed around violently, thus the soft edges and surfaces. There was a bathroom, accessible by a quick crawl, for vomiting and such. Ginger had seen it all. Because of this, she was extremely professional, asking permission to do anything, like touching my hand or gently broaching difficult conversation topics, yet at the same time she was extremely open, warm, and personable. It was a great combo for handling people ready to drive off the cliff edge of reality.

After an hour or so, Ginger and I sat crisscross-applesauce facing each other, I on my mattress and she on a flat pillow. She presented a mushroom tea, packed with psilocybin. She told me she would have a little tea to get more in sync with me, and I said of course she should. Who wants to trip alone? I finished my cup and after drinking her smaller cup, she downed the last drops in mine. Ginger was frugal with the universe-juice.

She instructed me to take deep breaths. "Just like, let in the air, and exhale really strongly," she said in her SoCal voice. She told me to center myself on the mattress and asked if she could sit behind me with her hands on my shoulders. I did and closed my eyes, breathing deeper. Ginger instructed me to make noise while I breathed, moaning or vocalizing my breaths. She asked if she could put her arms around my chest so we could breathe in unison. The rocking and moaning had an almost instant effect.

(Nothing sexual, you shush.) It began to reduce me to a child-like state, very emotional, very basic. The mushrooms were taking effect and, oh boy, I could feel this was going to be one A-plus fucking powerhouse of a trip.

We breathed and rocked, and Ginger told me to get louder, louder until I was yelling. *Ah-h-h!* More! *Ah-h-h-h-h-h!* Louder! *AH-H-H-H-H-H!* We rocked back on the inhale and as we rocked forward, exhaling, I yelled at the top of my lungs, and everything collapsed. The timing was perfect. The mushrooms hit like a freight train just as every bit of the artifice that we hold onto in order to act cool and be a normal person exploded away. I was yelling, crying, totally and absolutely letting go. I was a tiny fetus. I was pure emotion. There was no ground, only space.

Pain and experience that had built up over decades like geological layers forming on top of each other and pressing down began to shake and loosen. Good god, the pain! The loneliness! It had settled and hardened, had been ignored for years, and now it was Peter Brady's volcano, it was rumbling and lava was bubbling to the surface. Modern men have perfected the ability to dampen down our pain and seal it with layers of mental basalt and granite. We want and need to forget that the pain is there by telling ourselves how awesome we are on LinkedIn, until something triggers a volcano, breaking through the surface, and when it does, we act out, drinking, having an affair, or getting into a fight. I really believe most pain is tied to early primal pain, and right then huge chunks of my primal pain were exploding off the ocean floor and floating all around.

The whole time Ginger had been rocking me like a baby, a powerful undeniably maternal presence. My WASPy-ness* kicked

* WASP: White Anglo-Saxon Protestant. Pretty much *the* enemy in culture right now. Known for repressed emotions and heavy drinking. A joke I heard when I was young that defined WASPs for me:

Q: What do WASPs say after sex?

A: I'm terribly sorry, that will never happen again.

in for a moment and I apologized profusely, which made Ginger smile and say it was OK. I was exhausted and raw. I curled up into a ball. Ginger put a blanket over me.

For the next three hours I rode the intense roller coaster, drifting into different states of consciousness. Imagining conversations,* laughing at epiphanies and realizations, crying over losses, and generally being a giant hairy tripping blob under a blanket.

Ginger and I had deep, open, honest conversations. The kind you can only really have with someone you know you've reached a level of trust with, but who also doesn't know anybody you know, so none of the things you say will blow up in your face later. All pretense was gone. Love, death, pain, anger, loneliness—nothing was off-limits. The mushrooms were ever-powerful, and when I opened my eyes and looked at Ginger, she was otherworldly, sparkling, not only because she wore a lot of sparkly stuff, but the air around her glimmered, jewel-like, and light seemed to radiate from within her, shining out through each pore of her skin. This angelic vision turned hilarious every time she dispensed wisdom in her SoCal voice. "Like, people can totally grow apart, it's about the space you create for them to grow in, y'know?"

The psilocybin waned. I was clear and open. Now for the DMT.

Ginger explained that DMT essentially releases the same chemicals that your brain does when you are born and when you

---

* Or not. Some believe you tap into planes of consciousness where other beings communicate with you. I have experienced exactly this while doing Ayahuasca—search for "machine elves." When you see these creatures, they seem more real than a person sitting across from you in a café. During my Ayahuasca trip, these guys swam down from the ceiling and absolutely 100 percent laughed, sang, and communed with me. The nearest analogy I can make is if you've ever been scuba diving, sometimes you come face to face with a fish who locks its eyes with yours, and you share a moment of just seeing each other. That's what we did, except I was the fish. The mushrooms weren't quite that real or intense, but the conversations certainly were.

die.* After taking it, her patients often ask her if they are dead. Sounded scary but I wasn't turning back now. The psilocybin had primed me for the experience. I was open and accepting. So accepting, that when Ginger showed me that I'd be smoking the DMT through what was basically a crack pipe, I didn't blink.

She told me she was going to start me on a very small dose. Seemed smart. I closed my eyes, took three deep breaths, and on the exhale of the third breath, Ginger said, "Accepting," and then held the pipe to my lips and I breathed in the DMT. I held it for a long count of ten, then exhaled as strongly as I could. And not much happened. I looked around. Mostly I felt awake, maybe more awake than I had felt in years. I could do this every morning, I thought. Fuck coffee! But beyond the awake feeling, not much else was happening.

OK, said Ginger, let's do a real dose. Eyes closed, deep breaths, "Accepting." Inhale, exhale. And everything went far, far away. By everything I mean *everything*.

Time doesn't exist. All of reality is gone. I don't know my name. Everything Ted is no more. I am a tiny piece of flotsam floating in an infinite cosmic ocean. I'm maybe vaguely aware that I am a being. A being that faces forward out of a head, and that I have a line coming down from my head that is my spine.** Other than that, I am nothing.

"Am I dead?" I ask Ginger, almost dutifully. "No, you're alive," she says in the most reassuring voice I have ever heard, Valley girl

* Pretty much debunked, but this conversation did prep me for the following experience quite well. Birth and death are the best frame of reference for how one experiences DMT. One touches oblivion.

** Is this evolution? The spine showed up 500 million years ago during the Cambrian explosion, the biggest life generating era in our planet's history. Maybe the spine is the basis of awareness? Because I was all eye sockets and spine. If I were making me out of Legos, spine bricks would be the first bricks put together.

and all. She's moved behind me and is cradling my head, something she does each time I ingest the drug.

All of what I've described lasted for about ten seconds, and then everything rushed back. But in those ten seconds where there was no time, it felt much, much longer. Who I was, where I was, what life I was in. "That was awesome," I said. Ginger smiled. We spoke about what I felt, and then she asked, "Are you ready to go again?" Definitely. Now that I knew some of what to expect, I wanted to explore it more.

Eyes closed, deep breaths, "accepting," deep inhale, deep exhale, whoosh, ego death,* flotsam. And then the whole universe appears in front of me. Not just outer space. I am aware that *everything* is in front of me, and I am floating outside of it, observing. "Ginger?" I say, "I can see it all and I'm outside of it."

"Wow, OK, we may have discovered something for you," she said, as I came out of it again. "You feel disconnected from the universe." Oh shit. Yeah, I do.

And then it all floods over me. My relationships don't feel real. Everything is bullshit. Nothing really matters. Everyone who loves me will eventually leave. My success wasn't real. Everyone else is happy and I'm not. It's all up for grabs because it's all meaningless. I can and should act out whenever I want to, because who cares? Love isn't a good thing because it hurts too much and it doesn't really exist anyway. Getting fired was inevitable because I belong on the outside of the world. All social structures I am in are all artificial, transitory, and transactional. My life is and has been infused with pure nihilism: nothing matters and we are all alone.

* Religious studies scholar Daniel Merkur defines ego death as "an imageless experience in which there is no sense of personal identity. It is the experience that remains possible in a state of extremely deep trance when the ego-functions of reality-testing, sense-perception, memory, reason, fantasy, and self-representation are repressed. Muslim Sufis call it *fana* ('annihilation')." Yep. Accurate.

My whole life so far has been infused with this belief, affecting everything I do and think and know. I'm crying.

Ginger says, "Maybe you're a young soul, and your path is about feeling more connected. They say the most enlightened of us see the universe and don't feel separate. They see it and say, 'That's me.' They truly recognize we are all one with, like, everything."

I went to a school with a really good English department. They had us read some of the Upanishads, some of the earliest spiritual writing (around 800 BC). I remembered this part very well:

> It is everywhere, though we see it not. Just so, dear one, the Self is everywhere, within all things, although we see it not. There is nothing that does not come from it. It is the truth; it is the Self supreme. You are that, Shvetaketu. You Are That.[38]

Thanks, classical prep-school education. This thought makes sense. And being cancelled was the ultimate manifestation, the reinforcement to me that I *am* separate. I am apart from all.

This sucks. This profoundly sucks. Every damaged relationship can be traced back to this belief. Every selfish action as well. I am separate. Nothing really matters. What am I supposed to do about that?

Ginger said "You are doing something about it by being aware of it. That's profound. When you're ready, let's go again."

We go two more times. It's always the same. I am a consciousness separate from everything else. But I try to wrap everything around myself or swim into it. It all feels like artificial effort. And each time the experience is over before anything has shifted. It's frustrating. I thought I would be closer to some awesome spiritual truth, or feel good, or whatever. But the DMT is constantly reinforcing my separateness. It feels lonely on a cosmic scale. On a the-whole-universe-doesn't-give-a-fuck-about-me scale.

I ask Ginger if we can try it one more time. She thinks for a moment before agreeing, but I'm so glad she did, because this time is completely different. And the experience I had was as cheesy and embarrassing as it was real, so, apologies for the cheese.

Inhale. Exhale. Breath in. This time I'm not a particle. I know who I am. I know where I am. I'm on my couch at home (where I usually am). And I'm not looking at the universe. I'm looking down at my chest because inside of it is a big ball of light. And with just a thought I can expand or contract that ball. I can push it out so that it surrounds my wife and kids. I can pull it in and make it very small. Or I can push it out so that it surrounds all of New York. Its ability to expand is infinite, and when it does it never loses its power or strength.

Of course, you know by now that the ball is love and acceptance, and that it's in my power to extend those things outward to the people in my world or to hold them in. It's so obvious what the ball of light is. It's not even a metaphor, it's just a ridiculous, clunky, obvious reality. I'm simultaneously blown away by the sheer truth of experiencing the ball and its power of love at my disposal and shamed by how uncreative this vision is. If you had to think of a creative example of love blossoming from inside of you and expanding out into the world, the *least* creative solution would be a ball of light. But there it is. I'll take it. Upanishads, again:

> He who sees all beings in his Self and his Self in all beings, he never suffers; because when he sees all creatures within his true Self, then jealousy, grief and hatred vanish.[39]

"This ball of love is the answer to the separation, the aloneness," I say. Ginger takes this all in as if I've revealed the astounding news that the sun shines during the day. To be able to see that living inside and controlling a sphere of love and concern is the whole point of existing . . . is totally obvious to her. Yet she is kind and experienced and patient and knows that this feeling is new to me. She smiles at me like I'm a child who's just met his first puppy. "You weren't separate from that, were you?" Nope, not at all, and I thank her for that last go.

She brings me fruit, the first food I've had in twenty-four hours, and it tastes incredible. She leaves me alone for a while to relax and recover. I'm a spiritually exhausted, puffy-eyed mess. So raw that I find myself thanking the strawberries for being there, thanking them for their gift of energy and life. Out loud. I'm talking to strawberries.

Eventually I walk down to the kitchen. Ginger has made amazing Thai soup, and we chat. The conversation is still good, but it's not as intense and open as it was, which mirrors the faded effects of the psychedelics. We chat more, I put my shoes on, scoop my emotions up from the floor, and say goodbye.

Since then, that experience has remained extremely vivid in my day-to-day life. The way the brain sticks in its grooves, and being aware of how it sticks, was a powerful lesson. The self-imposed feeling of separateness is something I'm always aware of and working through—it's astounding to see how much of that separation is initiated by my shutting the world out, not vice versa. I'm working hard to lift that lens from my eyes. And the ball of light, yeah, it's in there. Using it is like going to the gym—it takes practice and routine.

Thanks, Ginger. You didn't solve all my problems, didn't erase my depression or halt my bad dreams. But the whole thing gave me an awareness of being outside of things, and an ability to shift that awareness. What I felt will never truly fade, and I can return to it anytime.

For that, it was, like, totally worth it.

Teddy

It is 1977. I am ten years old and very busy. I am the commanding officer of a tiny army currently grinding its way through the mud of my front yard. My soldiers are HO scale, meaning they are a little more than a half inch tall. The unifying principle of my army is that it is green colored. It contains WWI British Expeditionary forces, Indian Gurkhas, WWII American Marines, and others. My enemy is gray or tan or, weirdly, bright red. Sheer numbers have determined the sides of this war, and I have a slight numerical advantage, about 200 soldiers to the enemy's 125 or so. My co-General Jeff Miller and I have designed an attack plan: he is driving forward on the right flank against the tan soldiers, I on the left against the gray. My soldiers use twigs and leaves as cover, and Jeff and I dig hasty trenches for them when necessary. The grays are dug in deep in fixed positions. Although they have fewer tanks, they are bigger and more powerful than ours, trimming our numerical advantage. The battle is close, the outcome uncertain. The spring morning is warm. My belly is full of Cap'n Crunch. Hawthorne Lane is bright. Birds are chirping.

"Bish!" "Kapeesh!" "Pu-u-r-uggh!" Our sound effects are detailed and evocative. A well-articulated sound effect, plus the throwing of a stone, adequately simulates an explosion. The death of a soldier entails his body flying through the air and resting on his side. Side means dead. Standing means alive and still able to fight. If more men are needed for a dramatic incident, the reconstitution of the dead is allowed. "Tak-kow!" "Bra-a-agh." How do you spell the sound of a hand grenade or tank turret erupting?

It is one hour into the battle and we are slowly winning, but at a horrible cost. Tiny green bodies are strewn across the muddy lawn. (We had some large trees that gave a lot of shade, so despite my stepfather's best efforts our front lawn was mostly mud. Perfect for war.)

Then, a shadow falls over the battlefield. I look up. It's Richie Devons. Our neighbor. Richie is three years older than me and is often a friend, sometimes not. As the oldest of our neighborhood kid group, he rules.

"Teddy. You're a fag." he says.

Fag was a word we had all just learned, and I (and I assume many others) don't really know what it means, just that it is bad. Very bad. There is no homosexual connotation to the word, because we aren't aware of what homosexuality means. What we do know is that it is a very bad word. It has new, searing power. It cuts. It is currently, brutally, the Worst Thing You Could Be, replacing classics such as dork and crybaby.

I am staring at him. Is he just joking? Or is he going to push this farther?

"Fag," he repeats. He is smiling slightly.

The battle is over. Richie's one bluntly wielded word has ended it. The fantasy is broken. The brave soldiers on the cusp of glorious victory have become cheap pieces of plastic that I, all of a sudden, want desperately to clean up. I look at Jeff. I know he is no longer my co-commander, because he is looking at me with fear, anticipation, and dawning realization. Jeff has a choice to make, and Jeff doesn't hesitate in making it. Jeff is infinitely relieved that *he* isn't the fag. I am. Jeff's face tells me he is one hundred percent on board with Richie's mission.

Jeff giggles. "Fag!" he says.

I begin to pick up the soldiers and put them in a box. There is none of the usual careful sorting. Green mixes with gray and red and tan. Mud is not cleaned off. The evacuation is frantic and rushed. But it goes quickly as I do not, cannot, look up from it. I need to hide the tears welling up in my eyes.

"Fag. Fag. Fag," they chant as the clean-up ends. Are there soldier stragglers left behind? Probably. I'm sorry, comrades. We have to go now. One day soon we can return for your bodies, but we have to go now.

Being ten years old in Rosemont, Pennsylvania, is not that scary. It is a world of snacks and TV and tree houses. It is a world of riding bikes three towns away and not thinking about it at all. It is a world of throwing snowballs and mudballs and even rocks at each other for fun. It's a world of, "Are you bleeding? No? Then you're fine." It is not really that scary. But this is scary. This is everyone I know balling up together and growing teeth and turning to bite hard. The scariest thing there is, is now happening, and fast.

More kids are joining. Richie's sister Jenny, Jeff's sister, also Jenny, and in the distance my immediate neighbor, Bill, is walking toward us. They are all saying the word and laughing.

"Fag!"

I go into the house and close the door. I watch through the window as they walk away together, exhilarated. Their taunting has united them. Richie has solidified their allegiance, and his power, by expelling one member. Well-played, Richie.

I do not say anything to my mom. I do not say anything to my brother. I thank any-and-all gods above that they did not hear or notice what happened. The shame would be overwhelming. So much better to hold it in and keep it in my kid world. I go down to the basement and stay there the rest of the morning. It is cool and dark, the sun coming in only through one window.

At about 3:00, I open the front door and look out. The street is empty. It's warmer but still crisp. A dad across the street is mowing his lawn. I walk outside. Is it over? I hope it's over. I walk into the next yard. My ears are perked, listening for the sound of where everyone could be. Nothing. Oh man, is it over?

Two houses over, Richie's sister, Jenny, walks around the corner. She sees me and stops. Her eyes widen. She yells, "*There he is!*" Then, what seems to be every kid in our neighborhood floods around the corner behind her. Shawn is there. I like Shawn, but there he is. David is there. He is older and once we took a model airplane and pushed a heated pin through the fuselage to make bullet holes together. Pat is younger and I don't really care about him one way or another, but he is there too. These kids, they play in my house, and I play in theirs. We ride bikes together, and before that we rode big wheels together. This is my tribe. And now they are hurling every abusive word they know, smiling as they do. Their approach is so sudden and coordinated I realize they have been waiting all afternoon to do this again.

I do not run. I am a mixture of frozen fearfulness and every bit of stoic bravery I can summon. They run up and surround me. No one hits or kicks me, which is a relief, because then I would have to fight, and I hate fighting. I'm not good at it. But they do get close, screaming in my face. "FAG!"

I will not cry.

I have no response. I can't say anything. It would be ineffectual against their combined power and drowned out by their volume. So I stand, absorbing it.

I will not cry.

This is new. This is a new level of teasing. There was "teasing" before; everyone gave it and everyone got it. But this is new.

Richie has formed a coordinated mob with a single purpose. It has energy. It has direction.

I will not cry.

This is who I am, I begin to think. I am a fag. I am a loser. I'm not, right? But yeah, I am. I'm not to my mom, but I am to my dad. I'm not to my sister, but I am to my brother. I'm not to some of my friends, but I am to others. This is the way the world has chosen to tell me who I am. I didn't think I was, but the evidence in front of my eyes is overwhelming in force and noise and power and conviction. I am a loser. I must be. There was no reason for this to begin, I hadn't done anything particularly wrong or abnormal. I was growing up and becoming myself. So, the world chose Richie Devons as its vessel to deliver this important message. Inside, I feel an equilibrium settle. The narrative is constructed. A large building block of my identity is lowered into place, and cemented in very, very securely. I will not cry. I walk away again.

For two days, I don't go outside. I am still hiding when my brother notices that I am hiding. Being the low-level bully that he is too, he laughs at me. But then he offers some advice, which is the first good, real advice he has ever offered: "Why do you hang out with those losers? There's a kid your age who lives behind us. Go hang out with him." In the future I will take this advice, and it will work. The kid's name is Joey, and he becomes my best friend in the neighborhood. But that's in the future.

Three days later I am standing outside in the middle of the street. I see the Jennys climbing a nearby jungle gym. I walk over slowly, like approaching an animal that might bite. They do not bite. Actually, wonderfully, beautifully, they are acting like nothing ever happened. So, I do the same. Inside I am turning to a puddle of relief. It is over. It is normal again. But the cement is already dry.

Three weeks later, I am climbing the same jungle gym with Jenny and Jeff Miller. We are talking about the things we talk about when Richie Devons walks over. He looks at me. He looks at Jenny. Then he looks at Jeff.

And then he says to Jeff, "Fag."

It begins for Jeff. I do not look at Jeff. I look at Jenny. In a split second we silently acknowledge, we silently agree. Does she feel relief? I do. I am sad for Jeff, but I do not show it. If Jenny is sad for Jeff, her brother, she doesn't show it either. It begins for Jeff and inside I am so relieved. He will be in real pain, but I won't. It's not me this time. I am safe. I belong.

We, the afraid, dutifully join in.

Forgiveness?

MeToo: . . . and then he grew up a white man in a patriarchal world and made money and had every advantage he could have. The end.

Ted: What?

MeToo: We're supposed to feel sorry for you in that story, right? We're supposed to feel sorry for a privileged kid who had a safe-enough neighborhood where the worst thing that happened to him was teasing, something that happens to literally everybody at some point.

Ted: No, I didn't mean it like that and I'm sorry if it came across that way. It was about how we construct narratives that we carry around in our heads. How events, small and large, unexpected or mundane, sudden or gradual, can form our sense of the world. How they can beat the crap out of us for decades afterward.

MeToo: *That's* your formative experience? In a world where bombs fall on children's hospitals, where children get molested, which leads to drug use, which leads to crime, which leads to jail, that's your big formative experience?

Ted: It's not the only one, but yes, it was a big one.

MeToo: You got teased for three days in a safe, upper-middle class Philadelphia suburb. My god, how did you ever move on?
Ted: I get your sarcasm.
MeToo: Well, I mean, it's not real trauma.
Ted: I disagree. I *deeply* disagree. It was to me. So much so that I can replay it in my head instantly and vividly. I can hear the voices. I can see it all playing out. Have you ever heard the saying, "The worst thing to ever happen to you is the worst thing to ever happen to you"? It doesn't matter how it comparatively plays out, it's the worst thing. I didn't get to decide the impact it had, it had it.
MeToo: I thought you said impact isn't as important as intention.
Ted: Yeah, but their intention was mean as fuck. Their intention was to get power and to hurt so they didn't feel alone. I felt both sides of it, so I can relate. And I do get to decide the response I have to it, and I'm responding now with as much perspective as I can.
MeToo: Your response to it, when it mattered, was weak as hell. It made you mean. You think Jeff Miller knew how you felt inside as you were humiliating him? You were just as cruel to him as they were to you.
Ted: I know. I was scared and hurt, and I lashed out. That's the problem. I dealt with pain by inflicting it back on someone else. I think everyone inflicts pain; I don't think anyone can live a life without doing it. Especially in the brutal, anonymous world of social media. And in the world of 1970s children.
MeToo: Isn't it time people didn't get away with it?
Ted: Right, but what does that *mean?* Permission to inflict pain on them? That's just causing more pain. It should be time to find ways to decrease pain and suffering.

MeToo: That's the whole reason I started. That's the goal, and I've probably succeeded in ways that are impossible to measure. How many men haven't hurt women since I started? How many guys shut their mouths? How many damaging affairs didn't take place? That's decreasing pain.
Ted: I submit that, from what I can see and hear, in exchange we've built a society of fear and resentment. That's not healing.
MeToo: Well, we women were scared and hurt and lashed out at you. We couldn't build the impact we had with forgiveness. We've been doing that for far too long.
Ted: I know.
MeToo: Do you deserve forgiveness for treating Jeff Miller badly?
Ted: I hope so. If I met him today I would apologize. I would explain this story, and I would acknowledge what I did.
MeToo: Then don't the women who complained about you deserve forgiveness too?
Ted: (Long pause.)
MeToo: C'mon Mr. Forgiveness, Mr. Intention, Mr. Narrative. If you think everyone deserves forgiveness, and if *you* deserve forgiveness for mercilessly taunting Jeff Miller right after you were taunted, then even Diet Madison Avenue deserves forgiveness. Even if they lied. Even if they did it for fun. If you can humiliate Jeff Miller and ultimately find forgiveness for yourself, you *have* to forgive.
Ted: I don't know. It's really hard to forgive.
MeToo: Then what are you adding to all this?

Forgiveness

Two things will always be true.

The first is that *human beings will continue to hurt each other*. Albert Camus said, "To live is to hurt others. And through others, to hurt oneself." This is undeniable and happening right now all around us. The righteous rush guarantees it. The desire to split ourselves into either Good or Bad guarantees it. Misunderstandings, crushes, jokes, anger, hatred, lust, envy, and pain aren't going anywhere. So, we will hurt each other. Again and again and again. As philosopher and totalitarian historian Hannah Arendt wrote in *The Human Condition*:

> Since we always act into a web of relationships, the consequences of each deed are boundless, every action touches off not only a reaction but a chain reaction, every process is the cause of unpredictable new processes.[40]

Open the news. The first story is someone hurting someone, isn't it? And the next one is too. Check your email this week; chances are someone in your company is really hurt by something someone else did or said. Open your Citizen app. Something threatening and violent and scary is happening just down your street.

What is our history but a massive flood of humans hurting other humans? And we hurt each other differently from other animals.*

They did it to survive. Humans, we hurt each other for all sorts of intellectual reasons. To "own," to make money, to soothe our egos, to get revenge, to feel big, name it. The reasons are endless. But mostly we hurt each other because we are angry. And we're angry because we're afraid. And we're afraid because we're in pain. As my therapist once said, "Everyone's fucked up. Because everyone's in pain." And pain isn't going away. So, we will continue to hurt each other.

The second thing that will always be true is that *no one is going to invent a time machine*. It's not going to happen. And even if we find a way to mess with time, it won't mean we'll be able to send some guy back to talk himself out of doing that dumb thing he did. *Back to the Future* is a blast and *Primer* is one of the coolest movies ever, but a time machine is not going to happen. There's no going back to undo something someone did.

That leaves one course of action after hurting. Forgiveness.

"Forgiveness," as Sam Harris said on episode 273 of his *Making Sense* podcast, "is a fucking miracle. And we want a culture that makes us better at both seeking it and bestowing it, not one abusing us after every apology." It's what everyone wants. And we all have it to give. And yet it happens so seldomly. We hoard forgiveness inside ourselves like some precious resource we can never afford to share. We want it so badly that we keep it locked up.

I think most of us feel that if we forgive, we are letting people who hurt us off the hook. And in today's angry, judgmental,

* I took my son to the Museum of Natural History in New York. As we walked among the skeletons and reconstructions of prehistoric animals, a realization struck me, and I got a little dizzy: almost the entire history of every species of our planet is creatures brutally ripping into the flesh of other creatures. Everything around me had teeth. Huge teeth. Everything ate everything else. Everything killed everything else all the time. Life is born out of the agonizing pain of someone getting shredded.

righteous-rush-leaning society, we can't possibly do that or we somehow lose. Katie Herzog, host of one of my favorite podcasts, *Blocked and Reported*, often says, "The Internet does not do forgiveness." It's too tempting to hold onto that anger. The anger means we're right.

Open up the news again, and you'll probably see some celebrity asking for forgiveness for something they've said or done. It's become a daily occurrence. But because it occurs on the Internet, from one person to an ambiguous "following" in the ether, it doesn't have real power. Real forgiveness might just be, and only be, a person-to-person thing.

You, reading this right now, I know you can think of another person who's wronged you and whom you haven't forgiven. And that means that somewhere inside you there is a little ball of anger and pain just sitting there. Maybe it's been there so long that it's comforting to you. Maybe it feels like it *is* you. But it's not. It's a little angry cancer in you.

Advertising people *love* to say they want to change the world. We co-opt all sorts of problems and create all sorts of flashy creative solutions to say we are doing good. But there's one way to actually change the world that's available to everyone right now: Call up that person you haven't forgiven and talk to them. Let them know you forgive them. Maybe not in an imperious, douchey, "I bestow forgiveness upon you" way, but in a way that truly lets them know that you don't want to carry pain around that they helped cause. You aren't letting them off the hook; you're letting it go.* You aren't

---

* There is a great book by David R. Hawkins about this. I was talking to my Yoda, Kirk Souder, the wisest man I know, about loosening the grip pain and anger had on me. He kept telling me the universe wanted me to release. I kept saying "I can't." He said, "Let me tell you the name of the book. And just before he did, my five-year-old daughter randomly burst into my bedroom singing "Let It Go" from *Frozen*. After shooing her out of the room, Kirk said, "Ted, the universe is talking to you." "How so?" I said. "The name of the book is *Letting Go*."

giving permission to be hurt again by them, you're setting up a structure of love and respect that just might bring an old friend back into your life. Don't forgive just for them, forgive for you.

Poof, you just changed a little corner of the world.

I think conflicts inside agencies and companies and organizations will never be resolved in a truly healthy way without a mechanism for forgiveness. Right now, we have HR and lawyers. HR people are sometimes great, empathetic, and helpful, but sometimes they are the most gossipy people around, who feed off the drama. And lawyers, Jesus, their job is to rack up the hours and make sure their value is realized. You think they care at all about resolving and healing a conflict? In my experience, they absolutely do not. We need better forgiveness structures.

I think we all need forgiveness. We're lacking it everywhere, and the Internet is of course making the forgiveness drought much, much worse. Friendships are getting worse, and scarcer, according to the systems that measure such stuff. Here's Trey Williams in *Fortune* magazine:

> Roughly half of Americans lost touch with a friend during the pandemic, according to *The Survey Center on American Life.* And young women, who tend to form deeper connections with friends and rely on those relationships more, suffered more acutely: Nearly 60% reported having lost touch with at least a few friends, and 16% said they're no longer in regular contact with most of their friends.[41]

Obviously, I want forgiveness. I want to be forgiven, by the women I hurt, by my friends, by my family, by my tribe, by myself. I want it like water. I want it like sleep.

But I also want to learn how to forgive. And I want to get *awesome* at it. To receive forgiveness, I have to give it first. I want to learn to deal with what is, accept it, and let it pass through me.

I've been on both ends of that experiment, and while it feels good to be forgiven, it feels better to forgive. The thing is, it's harder to forgive. To forgive feels like letting a piece of ourselves go. But it's a shitty piece. I want acceptance. I want to let go. I want to learn to deal with what *is*, move with it and through it, and find grace. There's no other way.

Arendt again:

> Without being forgiven, released from the consequences of what we have done, our capacity to act would, as it were, be confined to one single deed from which we could never recover; we would remain the victims of its consequences forever, not unlike the sorcerer's apprentice who lacked the magic formula to break the spell.[42]

And let's not forget, she was talking about forgiving *Nazis*.

There Is Only What Is

On a warm day in 1987, a wave snapped the neck of my cousin, Mark Knight.

Mark was the coolest person I have ever known. He was the coolest person I've ever known before the wave snapped his neck, but he was certainly the coolest person after.

When I was twelve years old and Mark was twenty-one, he took care of me for a week while my parents went away. We did so many things I had never done:

- We shot a sci-fi Super-8 movie. The plot was about an alien who escapes his dying planet and invades Earth, finally destroying it. We created this destruction by painting a ping pong ball to look like Earth—and then lit it on fire. I wish I could show you this film. It's awesome.
- We saw a movie that started at midnight.
- We ate at McDonald's and Friendly's on the *same day.*
- We cut a jazz song at his friend's house. Mark had me sit in on drums. I told him I couldn't play. He said, "Ted, you don't have to know how to play. It's *jazz.*" I wish I could play this song for you. It's terrible.

Mark was cool in a way that I had never known anyone could be. He wasn't ever mean or loud or boastful. He was quiet. And thoughtful. But funny, observational, and wry. He always listened, and to a twelve-year-old that's amazing because no one ever listened to me. As one friend described him, "Mark was interesting and interested."

During that week, he showed me that life didn't have to be scary or filled with pressure. It could be fun and easy. And it also taught me that I wouldn't have to always play the role of dorky young kid. That a world was available for me where I was also cool. And it was coming soon!

Mark showed me that the world was available to me by just being cool.

A few years later, Mark was swimming off a beach in California when a wave flipped him over, snapped his neck, and turned him into a quadriplegic.

He was twenty-five. He retained all his mental faculties and basic, very limited use of his forearms and hands. And that's about it. As expected, it crushed him, and his family.

What kind of universe would crush a guy so cool?

I hated the universe after that. I mistrusted it. I railed against God. Fuck you, God. Fuck you for Mark's pain and everyone else's pain. If this is a plan you made, this plan *sucks.*

The Universe: Well, wait now, I . . .

Ted: No, don't worry, there's a turn coming up.

The Universe: Oh good, OK.

Ted: And then I became an atheist. Not because I hated God but because I accepted the absence of God. The universe didn't care. It's all random. Our lives, what happens to us, stars exploding and people stepping in front of buses without looking, it's all random chance. Who we meet, what we say, who we love, who we hate, who we hurt, and who hurts us, all random.

And while I lived in a universe where nothing really mattered, Mark began to rebuild.

He learned to cope with his day-to-day reality. He became more mobile. He drove again, using a van specially outfitted with a lift to get him and his chair in and levers he could work to steer, accelerate, and brake. He built one career at Vanguard, an investment company, and another volunteering with families going through similar tragedies.

And best of all, Mark found love. Her name is, appropriately, Grace. And the story of how they fell in love is amazing.

Mark lived in a house in Devon, PA, when he was young. When he moved out, Grace's family moved in. She lived in the same bedroom Mark had lived in. They met at a neighborhood party, and according to Grace, she instantly adored Mark, but Mark was older, so he didn't return the adoration.

Cut to years later. Mark is paralyzed and Grace is recovering from an awful divorce. She's moving back to Devon and looking at a house to buy there one day. That house is next door to where Mark lives at the time. They see each other. They talk. They go to dinner. They fall in love. They get married.

Do you remember being a kid, staring at the ceiling of your bedroom, wondering how your life is going to turn out? Mark and Grace stared at the same ceiling, albeit at different times, wondering how life was going to be. The same car headlights moving across the ceiling. The same sound of cicadas outside in the summer.

If time doesn't exist, like some very smart people say, then they were there in that room together. Unaware that they were lying next to each other. While the universe maneuvers and engineers the circumstances that will bring them together again.

The universe is always creating these circumstances, and we don't know why or what for. Bad shit happens and good shit happens and whether or not we consider the universe's plan indifferent or indecipherable, it doesn't matter. What matters, and really the only thing that matters, is what we do with what it hands to us.

The only place where there is right or wrong is in our actions. There is no right or wrong outside of us. Tree hit your house? Crops freeze? Cancer? Warts? That's just what *is*. It is what we *do* with what is that's important. How we take the circumstances and conditions and reality around us and use it to create, make, and shape into something. That's how all beauty, art, joy, and love is made. By accepting what is and moving on with it.

Mark could have, should have, had all the right in the world to retreat into bitterness, anger, and pain. No one would have blamed him. But he didn't. He took what *is* and turned it into something beautiful. And because he made an intention to do that, the universe nudged him along.

I'd been living with the idea that I'm in the wrong world, living in the wrong reality. I never should have been fired. I should be a CCO. I should be successful. I should be happy. But there *is* no other world. There is only what is and what we make out of it.

Mark died in 2022. He had survived eight heart attacks and lived many years past the time the doctors thought he could. The dinner after his funeral was full of funny, drunken speeches all focused on one theme: what Mark chose to do with his life, what he chose to do with what *is*, was truly beautiful.

Maybe

For some reason
I believe
Maybe
That we'll sit down together
And I'll say, I'm sorry
I'll say, I didn't mean to hurt you
I never meant to hurt you
I never meant to hurt anyone

And you'll smile
And you'll say it's OK

And I'll say it again
I'm sorry

And you'll look at me,
And maybe you'll say it:
I forgive you

And we'll smile
And we'll both say thank you
Maybe we'll laugh
Maybe we'll even order a drink

I'll say, wow
That was crazy

And you'll say, yeah it was
I'll ask you
Are you OK?
And maybe you'll say, I think so
And you'll ask me if I'm OK too,
And I'll say, I think so
I think I can be OK now
Good, maybe you'll say,
Good, I hope so.
I'll say, I hope you're OK too

And we'll smile.
And we'll be friends again.

And it will be over.

Every Saint has a past,
Every Sinner a future.

—OSCAR WILDE, FAMOUS CANCELLED PERSON

APPENDIX I

I May Never Lead a Creative Department Again, So Here Are Some of the Best Things I've Learned About Leadership and Creativity That Might Be Useful to Someone

I loved TV when I was a kid and I still love it. I watched endless hours of TV. I memorized the broadcast schedule. I *knew* TV. There weren't many channels back then, so we had to watch the least shitty thing that was on at any time. And often, the least shitty things were reruns from decades earlier.

One of these shows was *Bewitched.* Elizabeth Montgomery played an actual witch named Samantha, who was married to a guy named Darren. Samantha's powers were limitless; she could literally make anything at all happen with the wiggle of her nose.

Darren wanted a normal suburban life and kept telling her to stop the witchy stuff. Which is insane. Darren had a wife with the ability to do *anything, he could have had literally anything at all,* and yet his highest aspiration was to keep her at home in the kitchen.

Anyway, Darren worked in advertising, and he would come home and talk about whatever campaign he had to get done, usually by tomorrow. Let's say he needed to create an ad for Napoleon Soap or something. Inevitably, due to the magical powers of his wife and her crazy family, crazy things would happen, like the actual Napoleon would show up.

Watching this show, I figured out two things. One was jump cuts. Hold still, stop the camera, everyone stay in place, add or subtract an element, roll camera again, and *poof!* Magic happened! The other was that there were people out there *who actually came up with the ads* we saw in between episode segments. That was a job!

I found that job and did it for twenty-five years. And learned a lot. Like, every decision is made with a certain percentage of ego; it's smart to find out how much ego is involved. And how creative companies need dictators—that one person to be the authority figure everyone else complains about but follows. And people are all basically trying to do the right thing, except when money is involved; when money is involved, people will fuck friends and relatives over *hard* and still sleep comfortably. But mostly I learned some things about creative people and creative departments, which I still use every day.

1. The Burst

I rarely believe anyone when they say they've been working all day. Many people become masters at *seeming* to work, where they look like they're working but they are not really getting anything done. At my first job, a creative director told me he always carried a piece of paper in his hand whenever he walked around the agency. That way when anyone asked him to help with something, he could walk away quickly while pointing to the piece of paper, shaking his head and mouthing "sorry," as if the paper indicated something far more important.

People waste time artfully. They also worry about doing work, which isn't actually working.

I have a theory: creative people have about three hours a day in them for truly creative, interesting, conceptual thinking. This does not include polishing ideas, busy-work necessary to build Google Slides decks, or other things that qualify as actual work but not *creating*. Three (OK, maybe four, tops) hours a day to think abstractly and powerfully about a problem or opportunity. We only have a few hours to get into flow, to tap into our strongest burst of creative productivity.

The trick is to know when you are most effective for your best, biggest thinking. Is it first thing in the morning? Is it late at night? When is your optimum thinking time?

I've been asking creative people this question for years, and they either know the answer or haven't thought about it. The business world often expects you to be creative on demand, so most creative people haven't identified their burst; they've had to summon something whenever required. I suggest that whenever you can, flip that. Take a task and assign it to your burst time, not the other way around.

I use mine to conceive of raw ideas for ads or campaigns, not the actual script writing and certainly not for writing manifestos.* I use this time to sketch, and not fill in details in my drawings.

* Manifestos are long, rambling tone poems about how great a product or brand is. They are meant to capture a brand's essence. A good one can be quite moving. A bad one just reads as labored and ridiculous. Manifestos are usually two pages, with seven or eight short punchy paragraphs, three of which set up a problem or situation with the market or culture at large, and

This time is for thinking about chapter ideas, not polishing or editing. Every section of this chapter was thought up during a burst. Every edit and polish was done outside of it.

Know your burst! It's crucial, because this time is absolutely your most powerful earning time. A huge idea generated during the burst can win pitches or even start companies. Your burst is your most fertile creative time, and great creative ideas make *money.*

2. The Subconscious Takes the Wheel

If the burst is all about identifying the most productive thinking time of your day, an equally valuable time is when you *stop* actively thinking about a problem and let your subconscious navigate for a while.

Your subconscious is an ocean of wildly creative possibility.

Meditation is the best way to tap into it; it's like taking a long swim in that ocean. When I meditate, I can't often articulate concrete ideas from it (meditation is elusive like that, like dreams), but it works those subconscious brain muscles.

The best way to get the subconscious working on an actual problem is to *stop working on it.* Work hard, really think, use your burst time, and if you haven't cracked it, stop. *Actively* stop working on it. Live your life for the rest of the day. Play with your kids. Eat pizza. When you push your brain hard on a problem, then stop for hours, the subconscious takes it and plays with it, and most likely something will bubble up into your consciousness when you aren't expecting it. It's important to not stifle that unexpected bubbling with active thinking (which is usually just worrying) about the problem. Plus, you get to eat pizza.

---

one of which asks questions, which always boil down to, "What can we do about this?" And then four paragraphs ramming home why *this* brand is the greatest thing to ever happen to mankind. Manifestos are weird love letters. The best time to write one is thirty minutes after taking a Vyvanse.

3. Freedom Defines Us

Were you the youngest kid in your family? If you're a person in a creative job, I'd say there's a 70 percent chance you were. I love to ask creative people whether they are the oldest, youngest, or somewhere in the middle. I used to believe that "younger in birth order" equaled "creative job." My brother is a lawyer. He's smart as hell but not a creative person. Most people in marketing are the youngest siblings.

However, the more I asked, the more I found it's not the youngest, it's the kid given the *most freedom* who ends up more likely to be in a creative job.

Sadly, I think the oldest child bears the brunt of their parents' stress more than younger siblings. Parents dote on the first one because they're afraid of doing so many things wrong; by the third, they realize so much of what they stressed about was nothing. The first kid gets the ever-present handy-wipes and the massive overreactions when they fall; the third kid is gnawing away on the edge of the coffee table while the parent is barely awake.

For some reason I'm not smart enough to explain, this benign neglect produces creatively inclined minds. Ask around, you'll see, creative people usually had the space to fuck up, explore, bump their heads without panic ensuing, and stay out without curfew.*

4. Go Where You're Wanted

Joshua Bell plays the violin. As part of an experiment documented by *The Washington Post* in 2007, he set himself up in L'Enfant Plaza one morning and played six Bach pieces. It was rush hour in the

* This is personal. My brother had a tight curfew. He became a lawyer. My sister had a tight curfew and abused it, causing huge family fights. She became a health-care worker and substitute teacher. By the time I came along, my parents were so tired I didn't have a curfew. I would come home to find all the lights off and everyone in bed. No one stayed up worrying about me. This was benign, exhausted neglect.

commuter station, so approximately 1,100 people passing by heard his music over the next forty-three minutes. Occasionally children wanted to stop and listen, but their parents made them move along. Most completely ignored him. And some were visibly annoyed with their commute being burdened by the music. When he finished playing, no one applauded. He earned $32 in tips that morning. Joshua Bell is one of the best violinists in the world. That morning, he was playing a violin worth $3.5 million. Two nights before he had sold out a theater in Boston. Average ticket price was $100.

The takeaway from the story for most was along the lines of, "If we can't enjoy some of the world's most beautiful music, blah, blah, what else are we missing in life, blah, blah, stop and smell the roses, blah."

I took away something different. The people in the subway didn't care about how good Joshua was. Their priorities had nothing to do with the quality of the music.

Creative talent needs an environment in which it is desired, needed, and valued. If you work for an organization that doesn't value your ideas, your spirit will wither.

The most important reason you should take a job is that *your talent is wanted there.*

You can take a job for big money. You can take a job because it might seem less stressful than your current one. You can take a job because it makes your commute better. But don't be surprised if these jobs end up draining you of your energy, happiness, and creativity. The ability to do work you are truly proud of is worth *so* much.

Think about this before taking a job. Do they *really* want to do the kind of work you want to do? Will they really value your talent? I see creatives take jobs for the right reasons and for the wrong reasons all the time, and I can always tell whether they are asking themselves these questions or avoiding them. And who will end up being miserable. Like, $32 miserable.

5. Work Through It

When I was in ad school, I became really frustrated with a project one day. I couldn't crack it. I took a break to clear my head and went to a comic book store. They were having a book signing by Frank Miller, creator of some of the greatest comics of all time, like *300* and *The Dark Knight Returns*.*

As he was signing something for me, I asked him, "What do you do when you get stuck on a project and can't seem to make it work?"

"Keep working through it," he said. "Keep going."

"That's it? Just that?"

Frank Miller is famously cranky, and his cranky face appeared on cue. To him, my reaction was idiotic.

"I have no other answer for you. You have to keep going. There is no going around, only through."

Our world loves easy answers, quick fixes, and instant gratifications. Too bad. Miller was right. When you're stuck on a project that matters, that has weight in your life, there is only the way *through.* You can take breaks, meditate, come at it from different angles, farm it out to a friend or ally, but eventually you have to get through it. Author and life coach Susan Hyatt said "Don't get upset with the results you didn't get from the work you didn't do."

6. The Reflected Light Theory

Most creatives in advertising are deeply insecure. That's why there are award shows for everyone and every level of work. Even the worst agencies can win at some crappy award show somewhere. And the richest agencies flood award shows with entries to maximize return

* Frank Miller's art, writing, tone, and style is infinitely influential to the comic book world, and to popular culture at large. Today he is often considered misogynistic, homophobic, and Islamophobic, among other charges. These charges in no way diminish the genius that is *Daredevil: Born Again* or *Batman: Year One*. Without Frank Miller, there is no Christopher Nolan's *Batman*.

and shower their insecure people with shiny awards. Awards mean you get credit. Credit is the coin of advertising's realm.

It makes sense that most creatives are always seeking credit for ideas and concepts. They want to burn brightly. But when you reach the creative director level, it's selfish to want to think this way. You're responsible for others now. And instead of focusing on work that will get you credit, you should instead focus on the reflected light.

You can burn brightly by doing great work and getting credit. Or you can ensure everyone around you is doing great work, help *them* to glow brightly, and the cumulative reflected light radiating from them will make *you* shine that much brighter. Furthermore, when others see that your main interest is to help them shine brightly, they'll flock to you, ensuring an ongoing supply of light sources to brighten you up.

Rob Reilly,* one of the world's most successful creative directors, always says, "hire great people and get out of the way." He knows that if they burn brightly, he burns brightly.

When I started a temporary job as an ECD at Mojo Sydney, a creative named Alex Derwin** came up to me and said angrily, "You're probably going to be like every other selfish ECD. You just want to sell your own ideas, don't you?" I immediately shot back, "No, I want *you* to work hard and come up with the ideas. I'll sell your ideas, give *you* all the credit, and then we'll go to the pub. Deal?" He had a look on his face like he had never heard anyone say that before, because he hadn't. "Deal."

* Rob hired great people to do the Fearless Girl statue, probably the most culturally relevant and successful piece of advertising creative this century. That's a shit-ton of reflected light right there.

** Alex went on to become a great CCO, for which I take about 10 percent of the credit.

7. Beware the Good Meeting

This is the heart attack in your sleep. This is the silent poison dart in your neck. This is Dale Earnhardt thinking it's just a little bump.

The good meeting.

The meeting where everyone is happy, laughs are had, bagels are enjoyed, compliments are exchanged, and no one notices the work quietly dying.

"Hey, the meeting went great, the client is really happy!"

"Awesome, did they like the tagline?"

"No, we have to tweak that some."

"Oh, OK, which executions did they like?"

"None of them, but they really laughed at the game show one."

"So, what *did* sell?"

"Nothing, but they loved it all and said they were really happy."*

Everyone wants to go home at the end of the day and lead a peaceful life. Everyone wants to be able to pay their mortgage and avoid as much stress as possible. So, it's in people's interests to spin horrible meetings into good ones, with handshakes and glowing conference reports.

Don't fall for it. A bad meeting is where something didn't sell and no progress was made, no matter how it's spun. No matter what the "narrative" is.

8. The Creative Hierarchy

Every ad agency, marketing company and in-house department has a creative department. The following is a breakdown of the typical roles one can find and aspire to:

Copywriter: One half of the original concepting team created by DDB in the '60s. The writer is responsible for coming up with the concepts and ideas, and the final words that appear across every execution. Writers usually finish their

* This was an actual conversation.

work sooner than art directors or designers and can go drinking earlier.

Art director: Traditionally partnered with the copywriter. The Art Director is also responsible for the original creative idea and concept, as well as the look, feel, and flexibility of the work, its tone, and its longevity, i.e., its ability to remain viable through different executions. Often the quieter, angrier one on the team.

Designer: Short for Graphic Designer. Often partnered up with the Art Director or Copywriter. Primarily responsible for the look and feel of a project. As brands move toward more awareness of customer touch points and interactions, the designer's importance increases. Typefaces, textures, movement, and overall design systems all fall under the designer's purview. Usually has the least social skills and most side hustles.

Creative Technologist: An increasingly emerging role, a CT is a creative who thoroughly understands the technological environments in which a creative idea will live. This includes social media, streaming service quirks, digital boards and media. As we fragment, a good CT stays on top of it all. A bad one can still scare the agency into doing whatever they say because everyone is terrified of being irrelevant.

Associate Creative Director: A made-up title given out only in lieu of a raise or to keep someone from quitting. An ACD is considered not-quite-ready to be a Creative Director, but the agency doesn't want to lose them, so they slap this temporary title onto unsuspecting creatives to placate them until their next review.

Social Teams/Content Creator: An increasingly in-demand position, the Content Creator is responsible for consistent, effective social media creative output. Speed, flexibility, and prodigious output under high pressure are the key elements of this important role. Most likely to go to parties and switch jobs frequently.

Creative Director: A leader of the creative department. Responsible for ensuring ideas and concepts are not only sellable and effective for clients, but also interesting and award-winning. Must work well with others and make alliances with other departments. The CD role is one that should come with extensive training, as it is vastly different from being a normal creative. Agencies that throw people into the CD role without preparing them are asking for problems. It's in this role that the ego begins to grow beyond normal, healthy limits.

Group Creative Director: "We don't want to promote you to ECD, so we are stalling by giving you the GCD title. Also, we can't pay you much more than we already do, but people here like you, so if you quit it might hurt morale. Finally, we're worried we might hurt our ECDs' egos if we promote you to one, so like a plane that can't land yet because the runways are full, please accept this circling order as your temporary fate."

Executive Creative Director: The boss of the creative department. The ECD's primary role is to guide and shape the agency's work output, build the agency's brand through championing great work, be a public-facing voice for the agency, and help build the agency's culture through the application of passionate vision, while showing concern and empathy to all. The ECD's immediate role is to ensure all senior leaders in the creative department are thriving, and to be a sounding board and open door for the problems and opportunities. A very important role. At this point the ego is ballooning to an alarming degree.

Chief Creative Officer: A level above ECD, but a necessary one especially for larger organizations. Often taking on multioffice, regional, or global roles, the CCO is the creative soul of an agency. Hugely responsible for hiring in key positions, coaching and supporting their players. As far as the work goes, the buck stops at the CCO, even if they weren't involved in the initial birth of the work. Their presence, skill, and guidance should be felt and understood in all corners of the organization. At this level, the ego is entirely out of control, and as a result, bad *Ad Age* articles, annoyingly self-involved speeches, and other manifestations of delusions of grandeur are commonplace.

Creative Chairman: A massive wank of title. Newly minted in the last few years because egos have swollen beyond CCO. Stay tuned as a new stratosphere above this one inevitably appears.

9. Make Them Think It's Their Idea

There's one simple, powerful trick to selling an idea to someone, whether it be a creative director or a client.

Make them think the idea is *their* idea.

Take your idea, flesh it out as much as possible, and then chop off 30% of it. If it's a campaign, remove the easiest couple of executions. If it's a film, say you don't have a crucial scene yet. If it's an activation,* remove the ideal environment in which it lives.

Then take your idea to whomever you're selling it, present it to them, and let them fill in the blanks you created. Act grateful and enthusiastic. Now the person you sold it to will become an advocate for your idea, because they think that they came up with the best parts of it.

Tip: This trick works better when selling to someone with an enormous ego. The bigger the ego, the more they love themselves, the more they love what they think is their own idea.

---

* What is an activation, you ask? No one knows.

10. Sigh, For Some Reason

Here's a fun game to play if you have any doubts as to how ridiculous and absurd advertising is. Every time you read a headline about a new creative initiative from a brand or ad agency, add the words "Sigh. For some reason," after the headline.

"DDB Oslo Launches Social Collab Between Michael Ochs and Special K Cereal. Sigh, For Some Reason."

Works pretty much every time.*

11. Fall In Love

I thank the people who do the heavy lifting directly with clients and customers. They hack through jungles, they clear paths, they take punches in the face, so I don't have to.

I thank the strategists who climb to the top of trees or mountains to see as much as they can see and learn as much as they can learn so that I can know as much as I can know.

I thank the producers who figure out how. *How* is everything, and I'm bad with how. Solving physical problems, time problems, financial problems. These are problems I do not solve. Producers do, so I thank them.

I can't do any of that.

So, I fall in love.

It's my job, as a creative person who is writing, thinking and concepting** ideas to bring a brand to life, to also fall in love with that brand. To other professionals serving the client or the brand, its success is an entity to be aware of, to be dealt with, and to

* This wasn't my idea. A CCO named Matt Ian came up with it, but made me *think* it was my idea; therefore I love it and tell it to everyone.

** In advertising, "to concept" is a verb. It's not just thinking, it's creating ideas that will serve the brand, the brand's story, and the media that story could and should run in. It's one more word creatives use to inflate their sense of self-importance, like "creative" and "director" and "grand prix," but it's industry standard, so I'm going with it.

be promoted and utilized. But creative people, we need to fall in love.

We have to write lovingly about the brand we are working on. We have to craft manifestos to the power and beauty of any brand, whether it's a tractor or toilet paper, so our concepts need to be stories of why this brand is worthy of love, and to effectively write those we need to *be* in love.

I wrote ads for Heineken beer. I loved the clients, great people. I liked the company, great history, a cool, forward-thinking, global beverage maker. I *hated* Heineken. To me, it tasted skunky and awful. But it didn't matter whether I hated it or not. I drank tons of it when I was writing their ads. I ordered it whenever I went out. I made myself love the taste. I convinced myself it came in a gorgeous green bottle (it's fine, it's just a bottle). I discovered it was much more drinkable when it was super-cold, so I made sure it was as cold as possible whenever I opened it (yes, many bottles exploded when forgotten in the freezer). I convinced myself I loved the beer until I *did* love the beer. I found myself saying things like, "It's actually great, I've come to really love it." And we wrote some pretty good ads.

When I stopped working on Heineken, the spell was immediately broken, and all I tasted was a skunky beer.

Advertising is a dirty game. We must stretch the truth. Sometimes we even lie. Right now, as I write this I'm working on a brief for a large, consumer-facing financial services company. The brief is: We care.

We care. Really, large financial company? You *care?* I doubt it. I don't doubt it, *I know* you don't care. How do I know? Because when I asked for examples of how this company cares for its customers, I was given a short answer by a very tired, beaten down strategic planner: "Nothing. They do nothing."

We often have to sell something we don't like. That's the biz.

So, try your best to really see the brand as amazing. Think about it as a relationship you want to make work.

When you start a new dating relationship, you can either be in it for the long-term or treat it like a short-term thing. Or maybe it's just the fling of the moment. So it is with a new brief for a brand or organization. You can approach it as a hook-up you want to get in and out of quickly, a fun three-month fling, or tell yourself, *this is the one.* I've approached work in all of these ways, and I can tell you that by far the brands I fell in love with and thought long-term about were the brands I did the best work with.

I'm still amazed when I meet people on the client/brand side, marketing people who work directly for the brand itself, who are not only not in love but seem *exactly* like people stuck in a bad marriage. Discouraged, unenergetic, and looking to jump as soon as possible. This has a direct effect on creative work and team morale. Conversely, a great, passionate, marketing person or CMO is *the* ingredient for brand success.

As I write this, too, I am just hearing about a client who has complained that their agency "asks too many questions" when getting briefed. What? You're upset because the agency wants to know you and your brand better? Who says something like that? I know who: a marketing person who doesn't love their brand.

This somewhat clunky analogy to love relationships continues to hold when we look at creatives who did fake ads, or "scam ads."*

* I don't think people do this anymore. At least I don't hear ad people complain about scam ads anymore, except in the print category in award shows. Maybe it's too easy to have a side hustle that's creative and more fulfilling. Maybe people just finally saw how absurd scam ads are. Here's a fun test: tell someone who is not in advertising and marketing that there are fake ads done just to win ad awards shows. Watch their face. That's how absurd it is. I'm not against fake ads, per se, if you're a young creative and you have to make your own good work to get noticed, then good for you, godspeed. But if you're the ECD or CCO of an agency and you're still making fake work to win awards, then stop. Stop.

Scam ads were when ad creatives and ad-hungry creatives would invent ad campaigns they thought would win shows, produce them, and then get the client to approve them running somewhere once, almost always at no charge to the client. Client doesn't pay, ads don't officially run, awards are won. Like masturbation, it feels great and has a zero-degree of difficulty.

And then some creatives want that next brief, that Super Bowl ad, that next juicy freelance assignment. Then they can do something they think is cool. Key word being *they.* They're thinking of making a cool piece of work, not *the* piece of work only they and that brand could do together. This is serial-dater thinking. Because after they get their fix, they'll move on to the next.

If a creative person isn't there to truly love a brand, then like a relationship or marriage, things can get messy, mean, and selfish. Goals aren't agreed on, the future is in doubt, the relationship can't work. But when it does you get Wieden and Nike. TBWA and Apple. DDB and Volkswagen. Droga5 and *The New York Times.*[*]

Hey creatives, of any kind, fall in love. It's not only your job, but it also feels better.

After all, aren't the best songs love songs?

* "The Truth Is Hard." A campaign I started with other great creatives like Tim Gordon, the best all-rounder CD I ever had work with me. #timgordon #tedroyer #selfpromotion #backscratching

APPENDIX 2

A Cancelled Playlist

I love music so much. I might love music too much, so much so that I have to avoid certain songs; they're too weighted with memory for me. Music anchors itself in specific times and places in my life so fully that I can't listen to the songs that are too painful to revisit. Some songs fall out of favor, then circle back and become current in life again. When a great song, whether old or new, hits the right moment in the right way it's fucking life-changing and life-affirming. Cry-in-my-car-while-driving kind of life affirming.

Getting cancelled changed this. Songs took on different meanings. Old favorites reappeared with new things to say. Others I never liked before surprised me. Often songs that I thought were banal, pump-you-up, you-can-do-it, feel-good songs gained resonance, because I so often needed pumping up and good feelings. Mostly, the old memories that weighed songs down had less weight.

What follows is a partial playlist of songs that helped me and are still helping me through this new phase of life. Hope some of you enjoy this, and I hope I haven't ruined any of these songs for anyone else by including them. (It doesn't escape me that some of the artists whose work I love would cringe knowing a fifty-year-old cancelled white man is finding strength and sustenance from their work. Sorry. Music is powerful. Music is universal.)

"Digital" by Joy Division

This song perfectly nails the feeling that the entire world wants to crush you. It's grim and dark and spot on. Ian Curtis, Joy Division's lead singer and one of the song's writers, killed himself. So I'm betting he knew very well what isolation feels like.

"Too Young to Burn" by Sonny and the Sunsets

The first song is a song that appeared randomly in my headphones while I was walking to my first freelance job after Droga5. I felt old and useless and done. As you do when the world shits you out. Well, this song says no, you aren't done. Not yet.

"You'll Get Over It" by Lipa DJ, baked into "The Way Life Goes" by Lil Uzi Vert

Oh lordy, this song. It's so incredibly sad, and obviously about breakups. But it speaks to anyone with serious loss. It's all about getting over huge loss. And it rips your heart out when you hear Lipa's soft voice whisper it. It's as strong and sad and beautiful to me as "Don't Give Up" by Peter Gabriel and Kate Bush.

"Don't Give Up" by Peter Gabriel and Kate Bush

Duh.

"Up With People" by Lambchop

A great song about screwing up our lives. At least I think it is. I can barely figure out what this song is about, but it seems like an anthem to human fallibility, how we all mess up. Am I right? It's actually funnier and more meaningful and poignant if I'm completely wrong about the song, because I think the song is about being wrong. The ending is glorious.

"Let It Go" from the *Frozen* Soundtrack

Because, yeah, let it go.

"Serotonin" by Simple Kid

A song that asks, does everything really just boil down to chemicals mixing in our brains? Is that all we are? Pretty fucking great questions for a world hooked on antidepressants, like I was. Does our mental state depend solely on how the chemicals are mixing? Can one's state truly be overcome with a shot of Lexapro or Adderall or whatever the fuck to your brain? What a thing to think about when I first heard this, pleasantly tripping on mushrooms at my friend Steve's lake house in Canada. Thanks, Steve.*

"This Is America" by Childish Gambino

Yes, I know that as a white man I shouldn't say anything about this song. But wait, please. Throughout the summer I first got cancelled I played it constantly as a reminder that my problems were tiny compared to others, and the privileges I enjoyed were huge. It's unhealthy to compare your life to others if it causes jealousy, but if you're suffering, a song that brings you gratitude for what you do have isn't a terrible thing. It's incredibly raw and powerful, and the video is complex and layered with meaning.

"My Brave Face" by Paul McCartney and Elvis Costello (demo version)

Yeah, it's a dorky song. But I had to put on a brave face so often it took on new meaning for me. It was thumping in my head as I walked into my first ad party in three years. I was terrified, and Paul McCartney's cheesy lyrics were like a big mental Snuggie. I recommend finding the demo version, it's raw and often off-key, which makes it raucous and energetic and much more personal.

---

* Steve is the kind of friend any cancelled person should have. He sent me songs every day for months. Steve is great.

The *Soul* Soundtrack from *Soul* (Pixar)

Saw this in the theater with my kids and found Trent Reznor's soundtrack to be amazing. I think about dying a lot. And his before-and-afterlife soundtrack hints at an expansive, welcoming universe to embrace us when we pass. A universe I'm pretty sure is there, if DMT and Ayahuasca weren't outright lying to me.

"I Won't Back Down" by Johnny Cash

When you're cancelled, getting out of bed every day is a herculean chore. You imagine a world just outside that wants you to stay in bed, or better yet, die. There wasn't a day when I didn't want to pull up the covers and not move. I put on my headphones and Johnny Cash was sitting in the chair across from me, vaguely disgusted with me. "Fuck that. Get up. Face it. Are you a man or not?" Yes, I'm sorry. Right away, Mr. Cash. Sorry, Mr. Cash.

"Anything Could Happen" by The Clean

So-o-o, this is a song about heroin addiction, but let's skip that part. I take the chorus at face value. OK, you're down and you feel hated, but *you don't know what will happen.* Also, the raw punk instruments and not great recording have a scrappy fuck-it attitude. If the singer wouldn't give a rat's ass if he got punched in the face today, why should I?

"Khala My Friend" by Amanaz

A beautiful song about asking to walk with a friend, and knowing that you may not be able to, and you may have to say goodbye. Cancellation means losing friends. Actually, getting old means losing them, cancelling greatly speeds up a natural process. Friends are either of the moment, of the season, or for life. Being a Folk Devil means you lose a lot but the ones you gain are great, they like you not because of surface reasons, they like you because you've been through something. I like people who have been through shit.

"Chiquitita" by Abba

It was accepted Gen X opinion that Abba was a cheesy Euro-pop group. To me they mostly are, but they have a couple of undeniable bangers. One is "Dancing Queen" (daughter-approved pure joy). The other is "Chiquitita," a song written about a young girl hurting, from what we don't know. A lost love? A death? A breakup? We do know there's a wedding tomorrow, but the details are effectively left open-ended for anyone to identify with. The gorgeous, soaring voices of Agnetha and Anni-Frid wrap around the message of accepting pain and learning to recover. The harmonies and tinkling piano and thumping swaying coda knock me out. I knew the song before, but it hit me hard hearing it again in 2018, and I've loved it ever since.

And got me thinking.

There are hundreds of songs written about and for girls recovering from pain. What would any of these songwriters think of a man in his fifties being so inspired by this song? I can't shake the feeling that some of the messages of "empowerment" and "you can do it" and "nothing can stop you" aren't for me. What would a young female artist think if they knew a #MeToo-accused man was belting her song out in his car, feeling "seen" and gaining strength from it? Would that artist say, "Whoa, dirty grandpa, this isn't for *you*," and throw my iPhone out the car window?

Sorry, angry songwriters, music is universal, and its messages have a persistent way of working for all of us. Yay, Abba.

"Either Way" by Wilco

Jeff Tweedy's voice sounds like nothing if not weariness and hard-earned experience. Here he's saying: maybe today I'll understand. Maybe not. I'll try and maybe I'll fail. But either way I'll do my best. Yes Mr. Tweedy, that's all we can do.

"Redemption" by Nathaniel Ratliff

A song about running hard to finally find peace. A ridiculously spiritual, deeply human song.

"Today Has Been OK" by Emilíana Torrini

As far as I can tell, this gorgeous, soft song is about just getting through the days. One by one. Today was OK, I have no idea how bad tomorrow will get, but today has been OK. She may be saying it sarcastically, but I take it literally when I hear it, today has been OK, and that's worth feeling OK about.

"Stupidly Happy" by XTC

The world's most criminally underrated band brings a song about blissful stupidity. And feeling stupid went hand in hand with every instance of happiness I felt. "No!" my Debbie Downer brain would remind me every time I smiled. "You can't be happy. You're cancelled." This wonderful bouncy song says you should be happy despite everything being shit. That's the best kind of happiness, the kind of happy that nothing can take away from you. It's nominally a love song but XTC is too wry and cynical for that. Bonus song: "Earn Enough for Us" from *Skylarking*. All about freaking out over money, a big worry when your career is torched.

"This Wild Darkness" by Moby

I had to include at least one problematic man on this list. Moby was accused of being creepy. He's talked about dating Natalie Portman when she was a teenager. Yeah, gross. But I'm a true believer of separating the art from the artist. And if I can't forgive a cancelled person, I'm a hypocrite.* Apparently, so did the female creators of *True Detective*, Season 4. This song is about being lost in a spiritual wilderness and wanting to give up and die. At one point he talks about how the way we lived should be shocking to everyone, and that thought should resonate with anyone who got high, had affairs, or stole from

* John Lennon allegedly beat both of his wives. That's terrible. He was a messed-up, complicated, jealous guy. But anyone who deprives themselves of his music on principle is missing out on an incredible gift to the world. You can pry the John Lennon music from my cold dead hands.

people who trusted them. Go ahead and hate Moby, but this song is huge and gorgeous, and we all need light to see the way.

"Let It Be" by The Beatles

Also "Yer Blues." Also, pretty much anything by The Beatles. Also, the whole *White Album*. I don't really like the *White Album*. It's depressing and fractious and sad but if you're going through shit, it's really good. Its painfulness is more understandable when you're in pain. I guess it makes you "feel seen." Even a lunatic like Charles Manson felt seen by the *White Album*.

But back to "Let It Be." When Mother Mary comes to Paul, speaking words of wisdom, I mean, who isn't moved by that? OK, it's obvious and on the nose and all, but this preachy, churchy song is now a song that moves me to fucking tears every time I hear it. It's kind of the ultimate "Let It Go" song. And letting it go is sometimes the best thing you can do.*

---

* Maybe Mary did visit Paul. The Chinese have a belief that after they die the dead come back to visit you days later. Some say it's three days after dying, some say seven. I think the dead probably don't have much use for counting days anymore. But this happened to me. My mother died. Some days later, I'm not sure how many, I woke up to see her sitting on the end of my bed. She was smiling and radiantly happy.

"Are you OK?" I asked.

"I'm *fine*," she said, emphasizing the word in such a way as to say, *I'm incredible, so incredible it's hard to describe. Don't ask, I can't explain it.*

"Are you going to be around?" I asked hopefully. I wanted my mom's spirit to be nearby.

"No, I have to go." She seemed sad but only sad for me, and only sad for me right now. Like when you tell a kid something you know is awful for them in the moment, but you also know they're going to get over it sooner than they know.

"Am I going to be OK?"

"You're going to be amazing." she said, in such a way as to imply that I had no idea how good things were going to be one day. Did she mean in my life or after I die too? Mom didn't elaborate.

And then she was gone and I was sitting up in bed and it was raining outside.

Further Reading and Listening

Amis, Martin, *Koba the Dread: Laughter and the Twenty Million* (Knopf Doubleday Publishing Group, 2003).

Burke, Tarana, *Unbound: My Story of Liberation and the Birth of the Me Too Movement,* (Flatiron Books, 2021).

Daum, Meghan, *The Problem with Everything: My Journey Through the New Culture Wars* (Simon & Schuster, 2019).

deBoer, Frederik, *How Elites Ate the Social Justice Movement* (Simon & Schuster, 2024).

Dr. Seuss, *Oh, The Places You'll Go!* (Random House, 1990).

Harris, Sam, host, *Making Sense Podcast,* Episode 273: Joe Rogan and the Ethics of Apology, February 7, 2022.

Hawkins, David, *Letting Go: The Pathway of Surrender* (Veritas Publishing, October 15, 2012).

Hendricks, Gay, *The Big Leap: Conquer Your Hidden Fear and Take Life to the Next Level* (Harper One, May 2010).

Hornby, Nick, *High Fidelity* (Riverhead Books, 1995).

Huxley, Aldous, C*hrome Yellow* (Chatto & Windus, 1921).

Klosterman, Chuck, *I Wear the Black Hat: Grappling with Villains (Real and Imagined)* (Scribner, 2013).

Lukianoff, Greg, and Rikki Schlott, *The Cancelling of The American Mind: Cancel Culture Undermines Trust and Threatens Us All—But There Is a Solution.* (Simon & Schuster, 2023).

Merkur, Daniel, *The Ecstatic Imagination: Psychedelic Experiences and the Psychoanalysis of Self-Actualization* (State University of New York Press, 1998).

Murray, Douglas, *The Madness of Crowds: Gender, Race and Identity* (Bloomsbury Publishing, 2019).

Rauch, Jonathan, *Kindly Inquisitors: The New Attacks on Free Thoughts* (University of Chicago Press, 1993).

Ronson, Jon, *So You've Been Publicly Shamed* (Riverhead Books, 2015).

Segura, Christina and Tom, hosts, *Your Mom's House,* Episode 670 w/ Louis CK, August 24, 2022.

I'm going to try not to read anything about this book in social media or online comments.

If you want to say something to me, write me at:

tedroyer50@gmail.com

If you want to get a coffee face-to-face, all the better.

Notes

1 Jesse Bering, "Being Suicidal: What It Feels Like to Want To Kill Yourself," *Scientific American*, Mind & Brain, October 20, 2010.

2 Robert Karen, "Shame," *Atlantic Monthly*, February 269, no. 2 (1992): 40–70.

3 Bering, "Being Suicidal."

4 Freddie deBoer, "Dreams That Didn't Come True," FreddieDeBoer, Substack, March 25, 2024.

5 Andrew Doyle, *The New Puritans, How the Religion of Social Justice Captured the Western World* (Little, Brown and Company, 2023), 46.

6 Will Stor, "The Status Game: Male, Grandiose, Humiliated," *Quillette,* September 13, 2021.

7 Various Authors, "Mobs, Scapegoats, and Courage," *Free Press,* April 1, 2023.

8 Nick Gillespie, "How to Tell If You're Being Cancelled," *Reason Magazine,* December 2020.

9 Abby Aguire, "Taylor Swift on Sexism, Scrutiny, and Standing Up for Herself," *Vogue,* August 8, 2019.

10 Lindy West, *The Witches Are Coming* (Hachette Books, 2019).

11 Erik Oster, "Deutsch LA Fires CCO After Offensive Email About Casting Black Talent Resurfaces," *Adweek,* June 18, 2020.

12 Nellie Bowles, *Morning After The Revolution: Dispatches From The Wrong Side of History* (Penguin Random House, 2024).

13 Salman Rushdie, *The Moor's Last Sigh* (Pantheon Books, 1996).

14 The Quillette Editorial Board, "The Disgraceful Firing of Joshua T. Katz," *Quillette,* May 26, 2022.

15 Kim Elsesser,"McDonald's CEO Fired for Consensual Relationship: Is a Ban on Relationships the Best Policy?" *Forbes,* November 4, 2019.

16 John Revill and Oliver Hirt, "Nestle Plunged Into Crisis as CEO Fired for Hiding Romance With Staffer," *Reuters*, September 2, 2025.
17 Ann-Christine Diaz, "Former Martin Agency Exec Joe Alexander Sues Marin and IPG for $50 million," *Adage*, October 22, 2019.
18 Lindsay Rittenhouse, "New York Judge Rules Ralph Watson Can Proceed with Certain Defamation Claims Against Diet Madison Avenue," *Adage*, February 18, 2020.
19 Jonathan Haidt and Greg Lukianoff, *The Coddling of the American Mind: How Good Intentions and Bad Ideas Are Setting Up a Generation for Failure* (Penguin Press, 2014).
20 Lindy West, "I Rewatched *Love Actually* and Am Here to Ruin It for All of You," *Jezebel*, December 18, 2013.
21 Noor-Al-Sibai, "Sam Bankman-Fried Admits the "Ethics Stuff" Was "Mostly a Front," *Futurism.com*, November 17, 2022.
22 Scott Galloway, LinkedIn Post, December 2019.
23 Chuck Klosterman, *But What If We're Wrong? Thinking About the Present As If It Were the Past* (Penguin Press—Blue Rider Press Imprint, 2015).
24 Phelim McAleer. "A Big Mac Attack, or a False Alarm?" *The Wall Street Journal*, May 23, 2018.
25 Freddie deBoer, "The Rolling Stone UVA Hoax at Ten Years Old, A Time Capsule of the 2010s," FreddieDeBoer, Substack, July 17, 2024.
26 Klosterman, *But What If We're Wrong?*
27 Susan Sontag, *Voices: To Tell A Story*, Conversation with John Berger, Channel 4 (UK), February 9, 1983.
28 Douglas Murray, "Things Worth Remembering: The Indispensability of Men," The Free Press, June 16, 2024.
29 Lindy West, *The Witches Are Coming.*
30 Gurjut Degun, "Kevin Roberts Resigns From Saatchi & Saatchi After Gender Diversity Controversy," *Campaign*, Augst 3, 2016.
31 Maxient.com, website, 2026.
32 Dr. Augustine Fou, "Everything Is Listening: We Already Live In a Surveillance State, We Just Don't Know It," *Forbes*, September 11, 2020.
33 Grace Birnstengel, "Cindy Gallup: Disrupting Ageism in Advertising," *Forbes*, October 6, 2019.
34 Hailey Shafir, "Trauma Dumping: Definition, Examples, and How to Respond," *Choosingtherapy.com*, March 11, 2024.
35 Stephen Fry, "I Saw Hate in a Graveyard," *The Guardian*, June 4, 2005.
36 John Cleese, "Creativity Is Not a Talent, It's a Way of Operating," Speech at Grosvenor House Hotel, *Video Arts*, January 23, 1991.
37 Tim Adams, "Question Time: Noam Chomsky," *The Guardian*, November 30, 2003.
38 Numerous Sages and Rishis, *The Upanishads* (Penguin Classics, 1965).
39 *The Upanishads.*

40 Hannah Arendt, *The Human Condition,* 2nd ed. (University of Chicago Press, 2019).
41 Trey Williams, "It's Not Just You. Our Friendships Really Are Worse Now–And It's Getting Harder to Make New Ones," *Fortune,* February 5, 2023.
42 Arendt, *The Human Condition.*